THE ORACLE OF RASPUTIN

PRAISE FOR THIS BOOK

"An excellent translation into English, the Oracle of Rasputin flows very well, and considering the unorthodoxy of Rasputin and the historic intrigue involved it is certainly an interesting read. But the most striking is that it reaches into the heart of mysticism and ancient wisdom. It is most revealing."

— A.O. Kime, editor of *Matrix Book Store,*
author of *Metaphysical Cavemen:*
A Refreshing New Look at Ancient History

"The Oracle is a fascinating read. Professor Manteia has put together a lively chronicle of the mystic/starets/psychic/faith healer Rasputin, and has also given us Rasputin's personal amulets/talismans to easily divine our own destiny.

"Rasputin was murdered in 1916 Russia by those who feared his surreal magical powers. It took mega doses of cyanide, 5 bullets, severe clubbing and drowning to succeed. Long after being buried, removed and burned, legend has it that his dead body actually sat up in the flames horrifying all onlookers.

"Clearly Rasputin was amazing in so many ways, and the fact that we can now use his personal magic amulets today, which were given to and translated by Professor Manteia, is truly exceptional. It's one of a kind. A must have book for those who desire to foretell their future."

— Jeri Trannett DeTillio,
Actor/Copywriter/Director/Producer

THE ORACLE OF
RASPUTIN

MANTEIA

Translated by Paolo Benassi

KERUBIM PRESS

DUBLIN 2013

Cover design by Dean F. Wilson

First Edition 2013

ISBN 978-1-908705-06-8

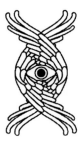

Published by Kerubim Press
Dublin, Ireland

www.kerubimpress.com
enquiries@kerubimpress.com

CONTENTS

ADDIO ... ARRIVEDERCI

A TRUE STORY IN A VEIL OF LEGEND

Riccione (Italy), September 1952. The long hot summer that steamed the magnificent Adriatic beach was ending, and it was enchanting to relax in this quiet and serene atmosphere.

The well-known beach resort was going through its usual end-of-season closing activities. The families that had made the beach so alive just a few weeks before had returned to their homes, and the variegated sound of Italian dialects was replaced by the Germanic and Scandinavian accents of the vacationers from these countries who used to come to Riccione at the very beginning or the very end of the season.

The beach lifeguards, with their wives and children, were beginning to disassemble the sun cabanas and tents, and to remove the parasols and deck chairs, commenting on the financial results of the season in their typical Romagna dialect.

The coastline now looked undressed from all the summer colorful furniture, stiff and formal, but at the same time very peaceful. Among the very few vacationers enjoying the last days of the season, was a well-known and respected chiromancer (palmist), who—during the summer—moved his office to Riccione, from his home town.

That was a very busy summer for him, with many clients, and many palms to read and study. Yes, study, because "Manteia"—this was the pseudonym of the chiromancer—had a very professional working approach, which made him very much admired in the resort of Riccione. During these last days of the season, Manteia was trying to get his well-deserved vacation.

Chiromancy, the way he performed it, was a strenuous and stressful job. His efforts to remain alone were not really successful though, as friends, clients or simply neighborhood hotel and restaurant keepers wanted to see him, with the excuse of congratulating him, but in reality because they all needed some extra help, a special "response" maybe, or simply advice regarding business or family matters.

One of those evenings Manteia reluctantly accepted the invitation from a group of clients/friends to have dinner in a local restaurant. At appetizers, nine persons were seated at the dinner table, but by coffee time a small crowd of local acquaintances was gathering around the dinner table. Dinners usually end up with conversations, and Italians like to discuss a variety of matters, mixing jokes with more serious issues, where all participants have something to say.

Because of the presence of Manteia, the favorite discussion of the evening was "occultism and divination," and the crowd was split between the people who just want to know more and those that consider themselves "logical and rational," and are in fact basically skeptical.

At the moment attention was focused on a controversial and complex issue: should one consider "true" or "false" the innate powers of divination typical of "supernatural" individuals? The discussion became very emotional, and disparate and divergent opinions were expressed. Several historic and legendary personalities were mentioned: Apollonius, King Solomon, Paracelsus, the Admirable Doctor Bacon, Pico della Mirandola, Joan of Arc, Nostradamus, the Count of Cagliostro ... and suddenly another famous name was mentioned: Rasputin, the Russian monk. Some of the most argumentative skeptics among the crowd indicated Rasputin as a strange individual, a swindling mind, a diabolic hypnotist.

This superficial analysis provoked the reaction of Manteia who—passionately—defended the mysterious and obscure Russian *starets* (a spiritual adviser in the Eastern Orthodox Church). The quiet chiromancer, who during dinner rarely spoke and was the unintentional cause of the dispute, was suddenly shaken by the argument and spoke out with unexpected energy. Showing an in-depth knowledge of the legendary Russian, Manteia described his life and works from an historical point of view, as well as from the angle of a divination scholar who symphatizes with a fellow human. It was a passionate defense and an analytical, honest review of Rasputin's personality.

He outlined the good and bad of the paradoxical Siberian, within the scenario of the decline of the Romanov's empire. Manteia's reaction seemed to end the dispute, when someone, one the most skeptical and aggressive, ironically said: "You future-tellers are very smart people. You can talk about the past and predict the future of your clients, because you know in advance certain details related to their life and personality."

"We are not future-tellers," replied Manteia. "We read and study according to the scientific method of chiromancy the lines of the hands and then give the interpretations written in those lines since birth."

"Yes, but also the appearance of the person can help you," insisted the skeptic. "For instance it is easy to say, for example, that Peter has always been a waiter." He emphatically indicated one of the waiters in the restaurant. Everyone looked in that direction and somebody laughed for what was considered a good joke. Peter, an aged waiter, very serious and polite, stopped for a minute, surprised at becoming the center of attention. Then, in a very humble and respectful way, came closer to the table, whispering in a low tone of voice, "May I?"

He then opened his palms searching for the eyes of Manteia, in the characteristic gesture of one who wants the chiromancer to read them. Suddenly the room was silent and filled with anticipation. Manteia looked with great attention at these open palms, in his own personal manner, studying their lines in detail. Then, calmly and professionally, he started to speak. "The form and the lines of these hands clearly tells that appearances can be misleading. Here we have a classic case. Form and lines of these hands show that this person has excellent breeding, and has an above average education. According to the chiromantic interpretation we are in front of a person who has a college degree, possibly a Ph.D., and has taught in University Colleges many years ago, in a far away country. Unfortunate events have caused this person to change what was the natural way of his life ..." Slowly Peter closed his hands and very politely said: "Thank you, you are correct ... please stop." Those present were astonished. Somebody tried to convince Peter to say more, but he excused himself and discreetly moved back to the service area. People were kept until late night with the most diverse comments. Each of those present was giving his own opinion and personal impression of what he saw. The aggressive skeptical guy, who had provoked the scene, remained speechless.

The sun was rising when the participants to that unusual dinner started to separate and return to their homes.

A few days later, Manteia was resting on a deck chair in front of the beach. It was a beautiful sunny day with a clear sky and he was enjoying it all. Suddenly, he felt a light touch on his shoulder. It was Peter, the waiter. "Excuse me, sir, can I have a word with you?" And, without waiting for the reply, Peter started to talk, slowly at first, and then at an increasing tempo, with a sort of unusual tone of voice. Manteia understood immediately that he needed to get rid of an interior and personal revilement, and was not surprised of the confidence Peter had in him, as this was normal in his daily working routine. Still, he understood that he was going to listen to an extraordinary story. Peter, the enigmatic waiter, told the story of his life. He often burst out with emotional and variegated details. He was in reality a Ph.D. in Linguistics and Physics. In extremely humble words he stated he had been a Professor at the university of an important college city in Russia in 1917. Unfortunately it was for only two years, while the tragic circumstances of those days ravaged and destroyed his family.

He was only 28 when he witnessed the distress and affliction caused by the Bolshevik revolution in his native land. He escaped to France where he met the daughter of Italian immigrants and married her. He worked all sorts of manual jobs, and never tried to go back to his professional career, which he hated. For him it was the cause of his misfortune, misery and bitterness. He and his wife moved to Italy, where he naturalized and worked as a waiter. Already aged, he was accepting seasonal jobs and was working in Riccione thanks to his fluency in foreign languages. Now that the season was over, he hoped to get other employment on the French

Riviera.

Peter was a tired and hopeless human being, waiting for death to end his sufferings, but continuing with dignity to face his daily task. He confessed to Manteia, who was listening with attention and understanding, his emotion on hearing the passionate defense of the Russian monk, Grigori Rasputin. Peter met Rasputin in 1916, the year of his death, when he was still the "omnipotent Rasputin," a few months before being killed by jealous courtesans.

Peter, moved by gratitude for the words that Manteia spent in defense of Rasputin, wanted to show him the generosity of the authentic son of Russia, by sharing with him secrets kept for more than 35 years. He told Manteia that his father Yosif was one of the last secretaries of Rasputin. The Russian *starets* had great esteem and consideration for Yosif, and this proved fatal to him. Three days after Rasputin's death, Yosif was found hanged in a wood. Peter's mother, destroyed by pain and terror, joined her husband two months later.

Now the old man was silent. The story was told and the excitement over. His eyes were lightless and somber. Manteia was now looking at the "real" Peter, a piece of refuse, crushed by desperate memories. He vigorously shook the cold hands of Peter, his new friend, in an overpowering and simple gesture of brotherly love. Peter remained silent a few minutes more and then, slowly and solemnly, drew from his jacket a voluminous manuscript scroll. "Keep it," said Peter. "You deserve it, because you respect and admire our Grigori. So keep it. This is the manuscript of an Oracle that Rasputin dictated to my father ... to be printed in intelligible form. The Oracle was supposed to be a present for our Czarina Alexandra. Make use of it in a way you think more appropriate." Manteia, now moved and astonished, whispered, "Thank you ..." Peter, handing him the scroll, said, "*Addio, A Dieu,*" then walked slowly along the waterfront, waving his right hand indefinably. "*Arrivederci ...*"

Manteia could not say anymore.

THE ORACLE

THE DISCOVERY OF THE ORACLE

After pondering a while, Manteia finally opened the scroll. It contained several handwritten pages and mysterious drawings; the calligraphy looked antique, large and irregular, and the drawing far from perfect. Manteia read rapidly through the documents and understood, or better intuitively "felt," what it dealt with. The document contained a sort of predictory method already partially know to him under a different format. The graphics, although incomplete and sometimes similar to hieroglyphics, were probably the easiest part. Most difficult was interpreting the writings, which were in an approximate French, interposed with sentences of unknown meaning in Russian. Some sheets were eroded by age, others worn out by coarse and rough corrections. Translating, interpreting and assembling the documents required time, effort, and great patience and determination. A person inexperienced in occultism and divination would have certainly failed. Manteia, using not only his professional know-how, but a tenacious character as well, was able to finish the task in a little more than two years of work. It was a job that made him feel like a medieval scribe. The final result was worth the effort.

THE ETYMOLOGY OF THE WORD "ORACLE"

The etymology of the word "Oracle" means "Response." Famous were the Oracles of Ancient Egypt, Greece and Rome. In those times, people from every country believed that the "Oracles" reflected the inclination of the gods. Oracles were consulted by citizens of all social classes to obtain responses regarding important business as well as common domestic situations. The pagan ministers used to "talk" to their gods via female mediums in a long and complex preparation. The medium received the "response" from the god and passed it to the minister, who then told the believers. If the "response" was favorable, then the reaction was enthusiastic, as the believer saw god being on his side. Contrarily the negative "response" was followed by total faith and no sign of protest or grievance. Oracles became popular and plentiful. Among the most famous: Apollo, Jupiter, Ammon, Trophonius, Amphisarius, Delos, with a special mark for Delphi, Olympia, Circes, Minerva and Vesta. Less known were Samos, Juno, Bacchus, Demeter and Chora. Pythonesses and Sibyls engaged strenuous competitions in creating prophetic works such as the "Book of Destiny" and "The Sibyllic Texts" of the Marcii brothers. The latter focused on Government Acts and Decisions. Examples are abundant. Homer reported that Odysseus evoked the spirits of Avernus and that Cassandra predicted the fall of Troy. Virgil wrote about Aeneas descending with the Sibyl of Cumae to Hades, where his father Anchises showed him his future descendants waiting to reach Earth. The ancient people of Egypt, Greece and Rome left magnificent monuments and temples to witness their trust in the gods and in the oracles. Other great ancient civilizations, China, Persia and India, did the same. In studying the document obtained by Peter, Manteia was able to grasp the methodologies that inspired Rasputin in the creation of his Oracle.

THE KABBALAH

This word is from the Hebrew *qabbala,* meaning received doctrine or tradition, from *qibbel,* to receive. It can also be spelled *cabala, cabbala* or *kabala.* The wise Rabbis used kabbalah as an interpretation system for key passages of the Bible, with a combination of characters and words. With the help of the kabbalistic science certain chapters of the "Book" were explained and disseminated to the new generations in a dualistic form: one literal and clear, the second symbolic and occult. By moving certain "letters" and replacing them with "numbers" corresponding to their special kabbalistic alphabet, the Rabbis were trying to reach the full knowledge of all the eternal truths in the Bible.

THE IMPORTANCE OF THE NUMBER 3

Continuing the analysis of Rasputin's papers, Manteia was struck by three drawings, represented in a circular format, and absolutely similar in the inside "characters." Only the external border was different. Manteia was familiar with those symbols, representing the classical talisman/amulet of Arabian origin, and the three words written in "celestial alphabet" in the external border. In his paper, Rasputin was reporting about a trip to Egypt, and the ecstasy he experienced in front of the Sphinx surrounded by the three pyramids in the Giza desert. The Sphinx appeared to him as a prodigious and powerful goddess, striking terror and respect, in the arcane silence. Rasputin reportedly spent several sleepless nights in awe of that ageless stone leviathan. The Sphinx symbolizes the secret of occult wisdom. According to a legend, she opens her stone mouth to reveal God's will only to paranormal psychics. Here Rasputin received the mystical intuition to compose the Oracle.

"During my sleepless nights, I was gazing at the sky, in a North direction, where letters and characters created by stars appeared to me," Rasputin writes. "Some rising, others descending, in a luminescent celestial alphabet. The oriental people have contemplated the prophecies in the amazing wandering stars. I have followed them as well, and I can say that there are three fundamental elements in the creation of my Oracle: Air—Fire—Water. Without these three elements nothing can be asked, nothing will be revealed"

These were the words of Rasputin, and in fact the three words seen in the external border of his mysterious drawings were AIR, FIRE and WATER. These words, engraved in the talisman/amulets, allow the user to ask the Oracle and obtain the response. Clearly the Russian *starets* was consistent with the theory of kabbalistic/esoteric science when he composed his Oracle on the philosophy of the number 3, the perfect number (Ternary Law) and its fundamental principles. There is, in fact, a surprising concurrence among the various esoteric, philosophical and religious credos, in considering 3 a number harmonious and eurythmic.

The number 3 represents the Total Power in his triune form, the Supreme Being as Divine Revelation. The synthesis permeating the pure esotericism affirms that the fundamental movement of the vibratory rhythmic universe is present under a triplicity aspect: Vibration—Idea, Vibration—Substance, Vibration—Sound.

These three aspects correspond to the three inseparable elements constituting the Divine Nature: Existence, Conscience, Happiness/Love.

The Divine Trinity is composed by the Father, the Son and the Holy Spirit.

In the sapient and intelligent expression of the kabbalah, the equivalent of the Christian Trinity is the Divine Triangle: the Crown (Kether)=the Father, the Sapience (Hochmah)=the Verbum, and the Knowledge (Binah)=the Holy Spirit.

The three principles of male and female androgyny, in total harmony, are: Balance—Expansion—Attraction.

A brief summary of the book *Sepher Yetzirah*, reportedly by Abraham, mentions an overall concept of the kabbalistic theory. The book teaches the existence of One God, as the order and harmony that contribute to variety and multiplicity can only derive from the Unique Coordinator. The book explains the 32 ways of Sapience by which God irradiates his light. They are made up of the 22 letters of the Hebrew alphabet, engraved in the sky, plus the first 10 numbers. His three forms are designated with these three analog terms:

- *Sophar* (*Sephar*)—the numbers
- *Sopher* (*Siphur*)—the word and voice of God
- *Saphur* (*Sepher*)—the Scripture and works of God

The Scripture of God is the Creation, the word of God is the Scripture and His thought is His word. Thought, Word, Scripture are one in God but three in Man.

To lead the 22 letters, the 22 Universal Archetypal, are three Mother letters: Aleph—Mem—Schin.

They represent the creative Triad of Mother letters to form:
- The generation of the Skies—Fire
- The generation of Earth—Water
- The generation of Spirit—Air.

Aleph reigns on Spirit and made Air in the Universe—Mem reigns on Water and made Earth in the Universe—Schin reigns on Fire and made Sky in the Universe. Aleph is Air as it is pronounced with light aspiration, Mem is Water as it is mute, and Schin is Fire for its hissing sound.

And the kabbalah admits only three elements, instead of the fundamental four. Earth—in fact—is Man. Fire is substance of sky, Water substance of Earth, Air, the breath/word of God is intermediate of the other two, and dominates and reconciles them.

Fire is Summer, Water is Winter, Air is Spring and Fall.

Every time and season has the same numerical positioning of Man and World. The other 10 numbers, called Sefirot, are divine emanations, forms of the infinite, with no limits in the future, the past, the evil, the good.

The ancient kabbalis recognized three spiritual elements in the human soul: *Psyche, Nefesh, Neshamah*; i.e. the sensitive soul, the reasoning soul and the pure spirit. The three forms of Soul correspond to the three Worlds: physical, intellectual, divine. So the world is divided in animal, mineral and vegetable.

Three are the basic expectations of humanity: freedom, justice, peace. According to the Far Eastern tradition the great triad is: Sky—*Tien*, Earth—*Ti*, Man—*Jem*.

The hermetic symbolism of Creation: soul, spirit, body.

The hermetic symbolism of colors: black, white, red.

The three phases of hermetic medicine: momentary action, incomplete transformation, total medicine or permanent transformation.

The Law of concomitant actions and reactions, known in the Orient with the sanskrit name of *karma* can be described in three moments: *Prarabdha-Karman* (karma in past lives), *Agami-*

Karman (karma in formation), and *Sancita-Karman* (karma to be developed in future life—reincarnation).

The three spiritual beings: archetype uncreated—divine idea (in the world divine plan), transcendent spirit—supernatural intellect (in the universal plan), and individual being—the man (in the individual form plan).

Three are God's names in the Jewish religion: *Jod, Jah, Jaho* (living God, true God, Saint God).

For the Buddhist, the precious trinity: the Buddha—the Doctrine—the Church.

Three are the Angels, elements of Divine Creation: Mikael—king of the Sun and the Thunder; Samuel—king of the Volcanoes; Anael—prince of the Astral light.

Three are the worlds according to Sanskrit lexicon: informal—subtile—coarse.

The Triple Temple: past, present, future. The Triple Hindu revelation: Brahma, Vishnu, Shiva.

In Man the number three is: head, heart, stomach. In the ancient Greek mythology the Universe is subdivided into three brother-gods: Jupiter, Poseidon, Hades.

Three are God's names according to the Egyptians: Osiris, Isis, Horus.

God is referred with three names in the traditional translation of the Old Testament: *Elohim, Yahweh, Yahweh Elohim.*

Three are the kabbalistic planets/stars: Sun—Moon—Mercury.

Three are the dominant planets in the traditional astrology: the Zodiac, the Decan, the Day of Birth.

In the ancient alchemy three were the fundamental laws to create the philosophical stone: to use only one vase, only one fire, only one tool and identify the three basic colors: blue, yellow, and ruby-red.

The Western Freemason order is divided into Blue Freemasonry, Superior Freemasonry, and Illuminate order.

The great order: Invisible Masters, Threshold Guardians, Rosicrucian Order.

The three classes: capitolar or red, philosophical or black, administrative or white. Also three the grades in the Martinist order: bluemasons, redmasons, blackmasons.

The Italian psychic Cagliostro adopted three grades for the rituals of the Egyptian Masonry he founded: brother, disciple, master, and three objectives: the reintegration of Man in his original purity, his approach to God, and the Spiritualization of Humanity.

The training of Zen—the Buddhist origin school—is in three phases: perfect morality, perfect meditation, and perfect intuition, and the initiation approaches: Zen—Sufism—Kabbalism.

Three are the steps allowing Man to purify himself and become free as well as spiritually powerful: wake up and overtake logic reasoning, use intuition, and reach illumination.

According to the brahminic credo God is triune: Brahma, Maya, Vishnu (father, mother, son—essence, substance, life). The legend of Krishna goes back to the sources: Virgin-mother, Universe-god, Trinity. The Triad, according to Brahmins: the father, Nara, eternal male, the mother, Nari, eternal female, and the son, Viradi, Verbum Creator. Nature—as product of the Verbum Creator—is revealed in three forms: Brahama, the spirit of the divine world, Shiva, the body of the natural world, Vishnu, the soul of the human world.

Three are the keys to understand the symbolic meaning of Genesis as found in the Egyptian symbology, and three the ways Egypt's ministers used to express their thinking: the first was clear and simple, the second symbolic and the third sacred and hieroglyphic.

Heraclitus also had three ways: talkative, meaningful, hideful.

Three are the Pythagorean definitions of the Delphi mysteries: know yourself, know the Universe, and know God.

Three are the doors open to the supernatural world: sleep, dream, and ecstasy.

Three the essential elements of divination: the sensitive person and his word, the observation of signs and material data, the pure imagination.

Three the steps in clairvoyance: retrospection, divination, ecstasy.

The Oracle of Zoroaster says: the number three is king of the Universe, the monad is the beginning.

In Babylon the Triad is composed by: *Anu*—sky, *Bel*—earth,

Ea—water. Three are the years of famine, three the days of plague, and three the wounds of Egypt in the Old Testament.

In the New Testament three are the Magi, and three their gifts: gold, incense and myrrh.

Three the names given to the Son of God after his teaching in the Synagogue: *Rabbi—Jehoshua—Nazarieh.*

And Jesus is called: Messiah, Rabbi, Martyr. Three the years of his teaching, three the Apostles to witness the Transfiguration (Peter, John and Jacques). Three the Apostles in the Gethsemane, three the hours, three the circles of Agony. Three times Satan appears to Christ and three times Christ implores Abba Pater. Three times he finds the disciples asleep. Three times Peter is accused and three times he abjures. For three days Jesus was in the Sepulcher.

THE CELESTIAL ALPHABET

The analysis of the Oracle showed the sapience and knowledge of Rasputin, covering various sciences, and in particular occultism and esotericism. One example is how the talismans/amulets have been set up and drawn, using the special celestial alphabet.

Following a kabbalistic principle, Rasputin used the word ARARITA linked significantly to the symbols of the seven astrological planets known in the ancient times. These planets are supposed to be very powerful and influential in determining human destiny. Rasputin was certainly intuitively aware of the existence of the Superconscious (foreconscious—subliminal) that allows us to master the prodigious force of the Supersensual.

All modern scholars of parapsychology are in agreement regarding the existence of a mysterious sense, belonging to the Mind's superconscious level, as well as the five senses. Inside the Superconscious is found the so-called sixth sense, better defined as Supersensual. It is a prodigious force able to communicate above and beyond the traditional five senses to the benefit of the entire human genre. The magical force is in fact unknown in natural science. The Supersensual can understand, reveal and explain the mysterious laws of nature.

In every person there are hidden magical powers, defined by modern parapsychology as "extrasensory perception" or ESP. The amount of information contained in the document received by Peter was clearly showing to Manteia, himself a scholar of occultism and astrology, that Rasputin had "intuitively" grasped a methodology, that, once presented in a readable form, possessed the value and the force of the ancient Oracles.

Manteia gave the name of "Phsycopitiology" to Rasputin's method. It is a system that allows the user to receive "responses" to specific questions. *Psyche*=mind, concentration and repetition of the enquiry. *Pitio*=oracle, magical ritual regarding the positioning of the Elements. *Logos*=the response to the enquiry. Of course, as in any extrasensorial activity, the personal participation and involvement of the user is required, to ensure effectiveness of the operation. A reproduction of the "celestial alphabet" created by Rasputin during his sleepless nights in the Giza desert, in front of the Sphinx, and of the three talismans/amulets corresponding to the elements FIRE, WATER and AIR, is in the following pages.

REPRODUCTION OF THE CELESTIAL ALPHABET

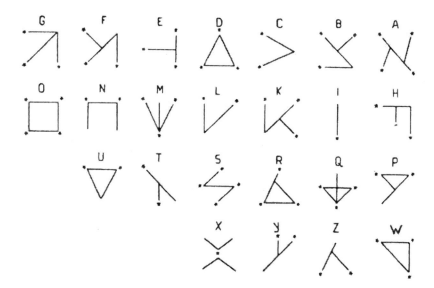

Reproduction of the Celestial Alphabet as it appeared to Rasputin during the ecstasy he experienced in front of the Sphinx in the Giza Desert.

REPRODUCTION OF THE
3 TALISMANS/AMULETS

The three elements to be used in obtaining the responses of the Oracle of Rasputin.

TALISMAN/AMULET FIRE: Reproduction of the talisman/amulet corresponding to the element FIRE.

TALISMAN/AMULET WATER: Reproduction of the talisman/ amulet corresponding to the element WATER.

TALISMAN/AMULET AIR: Reproduction of the talisman/amulet corresponding to the element AIR.

THE LIFE OF THE GREAT MUZHIK GRIGORI RASPUTIN

IN THE SIBERIAN VILLAGE OF TOBOLSK

Grigori Yefimovich Rasputin is an extraordinary and enigmatic personality, impossible to understand without knowing, at least partially, the customs, habits, origin, history and psyche of the Russian people. The vast Euroasiatic Russian territory has been invaded throughout history by thousands of barbarians: Goths, Vandals, Scandinavians, Bretons, Germans, Huns—men of different races coming from the Baltic, the Rhine, the Don and Tartars, from the far-reaching countries of Siberia and India. The greatness of Russia began in 1497 under Ivan III. The Mongols were defeated and destroyed by Ivan the Terrible, who conquered the Kingdom of Astrakhan and invaded Livonia. He was cruel and inflexible and terrorized everywhere with cold ferociousness. The Cossacks conquered Siberia. After him Peter the Great was the head of the Romanov dynasty, until the massacre of Nicholas II and the entire Imperial family. The country of Russia, particularly at the time of Rasputin, was a mysterious and indecipherable place, consisting of several races and cultures, religious beliefs and superstitions, influenced by a sort of mysticism in all aspects of life. The Russian people seemed to be always waiting for a messianic leader in direct communication with the Invisible and the Divine.

Given this scenario, the "phenomenon of Rasputin" was able to touch the soul of the Russian people, from the Emperor's family to the simple *muzhik*. Grigori Yefimovich Rasputin, son of a peasant coach driver, Yefim Andrejevich, was born in 1871 in the village of Pokrowskoje, in the poor district of Tobolsk, in West Siberia, on the Tura river. Grigori (Grischa was his boyish name) spent his early life in his father's house. Grischa's father, a peasant who had a small horse breeding business, was considered the "wise man" of the village, even though he could not read or write. Often, in his stable, community meetings took place to decide in the name of the village or simply to share information and conversation. Grischa, a bright and rebellious young man, enjoyed his moments of relaxation among the father's horses. His best friend was a horse to which he used to talk as one would to a companion. He liked freedom, light, sounds and fresh air. He was also very religious and an avid reader of the Bible and the life of Christ.

The Scriptures, with their illustrations, moved his imagination and creativity, and the protagonists became his heroes and a model of beauty, honor and mystery. Premonitions of an uncommon life appeared precociously in Grischa's life. He was fascinated by the stories of the errant *starets*, pilgrims charged with inexplicable powers, capable of molding a person's soul and will to a point where they achieved full control of anyone's personality to meet peace, freedom, and health. When he was eight a tragic incident affected the growing spiritual life of Grischa. His older brother, Mischa, while playing, fell in the waters of the Tura river. Grischa jumped immediately into the water, trying desperately to save his brother. The current was too strong and both boys would have died without the providential intervention of a local farmer. Unfortunately Mischa died of pneumonia a few days later and Grischa became seriously ill for a long time. The young man, once exuberantly healthy, was transformed into a pale and fragile boy. The sickness and the subsequent long convalescence created an odd sensitivity in Grischa, which slowly became the extraordinary power of intuition and divination.

He was about 12 when a singular incident happened in the village of Pokrowskoje. A poor *muzhik* had been robbed of his only horse. This horse was the only means of subsistence for the man, and at the house of Rasputin's father the robbery was commented upon and disapproved of. Grischa had been in bed for days suffering with fever. Resting by the fireplace he was listening to the grown-up's conversation. Suddenly his trembling voice was heard: "The robber ... is Ivan ... the Red." Those words were received by general surprise. Ivan the Red was a rich merchant, well known and respected, and nobody could suspect him. Later, during the night, Ivan the Red was seen trying to let the poor man's horse escape from his stable. Everybody thought that God had spoken through Rasputin's voice.

And year after year these extraordinary phenomena of clairvoyance became routine. People went to see Rasputin to ask questions, discuss problems, and talk about health. Rasputin listened silently and then provided his advice, with wise and discerning knowledge. He cured the sick, settled disputes. He implored and ordered, requested and obtained. Grigori was also very powerful with animals and trained wild horses in a very simple and effective way, until they became obedient and friendly. Was he really super powerful or only clever? Victor, the stable keeper told several times this story:

Yefim owned a stallion that was so furious people believed that it should be killed. The big horse was a terror. He kept kicking around, even when they were bringing food. "Wait," said Grischa one day, "let me go into the stable." A small crowd followed cautiously. When the top door was open, the stallion, his ears lowered and his mouth foamy, rushed to the door neighing furiously. Everybody ran away except Grischa, who stopped in front of the stallion's face, and started to talk to him in a calm and soothing tone of voice. Nobody could hear the words, nor their meaning. Rasputin talked to the stallion for a while, until the animal, apparently relaxed, went back to eating his forage. Then Grischa opened the door completely and entered the stable. Continuing to talk in the same calm tone of voice, he neared the stallion and caressed him on his neck. The stallion violently shook but continued to eat. After a while he was totally tamed and quietly joined the other horses.

Another unusual event happened to Rasputin when he was nearly 20. His father had been lying sick in bed for more than ten days and the village's doctor was helplessly trying to cure him. One evening Grigori fell in a trance and revealed to the amazed doctor the nature of the illness and how to cure it.

At the age of 20 Rasputin married Fedorovna Preskovia, a wealthy and beautiful village girl, with whom he had been engaged for a year. They went to live in his father's house. Now Rasputin was wearing a thick reddish beard that made him look like a religious person. He was healing sick people and taming horses with ease, and his reputation started to spread outside his district. But Grigori was not satisfied. A feeling of restlessness, of unfulfillment, very difficult for him to control, possessed him. He felt an unconscious desire for knowledge, for experiencing. He seemed to be constantly looking for something that was beyond him. Silent spirits accompanied him and he was questioning them, without reply. In his life there was silence and no guiding light. Meanwhile he was working as a coachman, like his father. He was transporting goods and passengers from Tobolsk to Tiumen and Werchoturje, at the foot of the Ural Mountains. Although a married man, he had a lustful extramarital sex life. He was known as a very heavy drinker and womanizer.

LIFE AND LUST AT THE MONASTERY

Then one day the great light Rasputin was looking for finally appeared. When he was about 30 he met a student from the Ecclesiastic Academy, the young theosophist Miletj Saborowkj, whom he used to take by coach to the convent of Werchoturje. This young man was a member of an unusual Confraternity called "Men of God." The Russian Orthodox Church considered these people apostates. Grigori did not return home and stayed at the Monastery where he came to know better the Confraternity that is also called "The Sect of Flagellants." They were in penitence at the Monastery, hoping to be readopted by the Mother Church. The sect was founded 200 years earlier by Danilo Filipich, who wrote: "Keep my Laws secret, never reveal them not even to your father or your mother. Be firm and silent even if tortured with fire and whip." In practice, to reach the Divine Communion, these people went through all sorts of perversions and lust. In the woodland and forests they used to dance furiously, and their leader whipped those who were not participating. Exhausted, they would lose consciousness, be taken over by ecstasy and vertigo, and abandon themselves to orgiastic and debauched rituals, believed to be protected by the Divine Grace. The sensual strength and intemperate character of Rasputin made him an ideal "candidate" to receive the divine grace and entrance into the sect. Here he found the fulfillment of his needs and of his abnormal imagination. Miletj became the source from where Rasputin's thirst was appeased. The young theologian found in Rasputin a rustic but enthusiastic brother, rich in intuition and quick to understand.

Their encounter changed Rasputin's life. In the Monastery he also met father Makary, an old and wise monk who became his master. Makary was so old that nobody knew his true age, but his mind was clear and fertile and he possessed supernatural wisdom. Father Makary thought Rasputin all the sublime disciplines of the Oriental occultism and became his mentor and guide. Rasputin remained several years in the Monastery, where his strong memory made him conversant with the encyclopedic knowledge. At the same time, the rituals and customs of the sect entered his personality and took over completely his already predisposed mental and sensual nature. Grigori had the power to duplicate his persona. The spiritual "ego" was moving above and beyond the boundaries of human nature and flew on the top of the psyche, guiding normal intelligence and pushing the "hypersensitivity" to excesses of fanaticism. But the material "ego" was down to earth, desperately attached to sensual pleasures, prisoner of female beauty.

The strong and complex nature of Rasputin found a natural way of life in the rituals of the sect, abjured by the traditional Church. Rasputin had the ability to talk to people's souls, providing a message of faith and hope. Yet at any moment his warm and fascinating look would change and his eyes would be full of beastly passion and sexual desire. He could not resist the temptation to possess a woman, and only a few women had the strength to resist him. Most women offered their body to him for veneration, for fear, for lust, for exaltation, for need, for love, for hate. The irresistible attraction for women went together with an insatiable gluttony. In particular he loved fish cooked with exciting spices together with warm Spanish wine. Usually a good dinner ended with an irresistible inclination for dancing. When he started to dance one of the many dances of his great land, his face was transfigured and his body became charged with an interior force. The most difficult dancing steps came out easy, often solemn. At such times he looked transcendental and pure, like he was part of another world. It was impossible to recognize the vicious individual seen before.

Was all this a fabrication, and Rasputin just a mere comedian? We have reason to believe that Rasputin was in good faith and the duplication of his personality just an aspect of an extraordinary nature.

Father Makarj believed in the theory of reincarnation and explained it to Rasputin, who was an attentive and intelligent pupil. The ancient pagan doctrines coming from Asia and dealing with metempsychosis and reincarnation have been recently recalled by scholars of occultism and theosophy. According to reincarnation, Man is supposed to rebirth several times and his soul to move from one body to another till reaching perfection.

This doctrine originates mainly from the Indian and Buddhist tradition, but according to theosophy and spiritualism the reincarnation cannot take place in an animal's body. The reincarnation of the souls can only manifest in conditions of progressive existence, in this world or others, to represent a continuous ascent to the triumph of Spirit.

The science called Entelechy, which has the objective of studying and diffusing the knowledge of the *Enteles*, the complete, reminds us that the law of reincarnation is not only the proof of mercy, but also the perfect justice of the Father. It differs from human justice because the condemnation of the sinners is not *ab aeterno*, but it is such that, after the expiation, the sinners may return to the original purity.

But let us go back to Rasputin's life. Grigori Rasputin was no longer the miserable *muzhik* from the faraway district of Tobolsk. Time, with its unstoppable flow, had caused his maturation. His physical strength, typical of the people of his geographic area, and his will, stubborn and tough, forced him to strive against the desperate misery of his youth. He lived for more than 30 years among his people, where he learned to sacrifice himself, to suffer and to hope.

One day he went to see father Makarj and ask for his blessing. He wanted to leave the Monastery. From Werchoturje, Grigori went directly to see his relatives and say farewell to them. Rasputin wanted to be a *starets stranniki*, a saint pilgrim, because he felt purified through sin. These errant preachers were well known in Russia, and always found assistance and restoration when needed. They were commonly known as *Podpolnik*, people of the family room, literally of the place under the staircases, because this was the shelter usually given to them in the houses they visited.

In his travelling Rasputin had the opportunity to know even better the characteristics of the Russian people and soul. During his wandering he was fully initiated into the secret practices of his sect up to the so-called "mystical death," the terminal and final act of the obscene ceremony. He wore a white shirt, the vest of spirits and angels. He danced and sung to the light of twelve black candles, until his body was completely frozen, the tongue paralyzed, the mind distorted and his body whipped with the lash made by willow-tree leaves.

Then he took part in the "sublime affray," an activity where monstrous coupling was the rule. His pilgrimage lasted more than three years. His father, mother, wife and sons were totally unaware of what he did. Words coming from travelers reported to have seen him in feasts and in ceremonies, where he was referred to as "the new *starets*." He was helping the fishermen of the high Tura Valley. He was teaching rituals and sacred hymns. He was involved in magic acts with young women in the forests. He was creating crosses with trees and was praying together with his disciples, again mainly women. Songs, dances, and lust were all part of the "divine service."

Grigori, being radically transformed by his religious fervor, caused surprising recoveries. To the *muzhiks* that thanked him, he replied, "God healed you, I am only His servant." The Pope Ivan of Kronstad became interested in Rasputin because of his reputation as "healer" and wanted to meet him. The Pope spoke with him in the Cathedral of St. Petersburg and told him, "Son, I have felt your presence. You bring with you the flame of true religion." Rasputin knew the Bible by heart and gave his own interpretation to the Sacred Scriptures. At that time the Orthodox Church was opposed to lay men reading the Bible.

One day by a sudden decision, as he used to do, Rasputin returned home and asked hospitality of his wife, like a normal *stranniki*. In the silence of the house he started to pray and continued for several days. In the village they considered him a *starets* as he was saying "saint" words. His biggest fans were the local women falling in love to him, in a mixture of mother-like affection and mystical fervor. The *starets* Rasputin, in an underground chapel, was healing the sick people coming from the villages. His most remarkable feature, after his eyes, was his voice. His voice was warm and modulated and resembled an organ playing softly or the Caucasian velvets. He spoke, he reassured, and he gave guidance. The sick person calmed down, forgot the pain and relaxed.

The number of sick people visiting Rasputin was increasing day by day, and the practice kept him very busy and started to cause unusual physical reactions. His face assumed a sort of earthly color and caused him to look tired and in suffering. From time to time he stopped his work. "Bring me tea, a lot of tea, and very hot." At the end of his healing, Rasputin fell into a strange trance lasting for hours. It was like a nervous reaction, a coma-like condition, very similar to death.

It is known that the Tibetan Lamas exercise their great healing by transferring into themselves the sickness of the person they are in process of curing. Their physical strength made it possible for them to get better and finally to get rid of the sickness.

Probably Rasputin was going through something like this. He was, undoubtedly, in possession of a charge of so called "beneficial waves." These are special irradiations existing in supernatural individuals who can act therapeutically and thaumaturgically. These individuals can control a personal fluid that is transferred into the sick person, or in a part of his body, by hand imposition. The fluid can have instant effect and heal on the spot. A related infusion is gained by the presence of personal magnetism.

The modern esoteric science defines "mana" as this original strength of healing. It is strength deriving from animal energy and is formed by electric energies coming from the soul, which has power unknown to human science.

The force is supposed to have three grades:

1. Low mana: related to natural objects, from mineral crystals to the human organism.

2. Medium mana: irradiated from the reasoning centers of the human mind.

3. Sublime mana: proceeding from the supernormal faculties of the mind and causing supernatural reactions.

Rasputin will be a fascinating case study for modern parapsychology. The village's Pope, Father Pjotr, called Rasputin a damned apostate and condemned those who listened to and believed him. This excommunication resulted in increasing the number of visitors coming from everywhere. A policeman, sent by the Pope, came back converted. The village people told that Rasputin had the power to stop the rain when it was damaging the harvest, and to make the rain when the earth needed it.

The reputation of this new *starets* rapidly spread beyond the province. Everybody called him *starets*, but in fact he was only a *muzhik*. He never received any religious order and was called *starets* only by respect. Grigori continued to produce surprising prodigies and then he retired to pray, in a mystical and silent way. After this ritual he used to walk into the streets and move among the crowd in a slow and solemn behavior. His eyes showed happiness, serenity and benignity. The farmers fell at his feet, kissing his hands and his vest.

TO THE COURT OF RUSSIA: SPLENDOUR AND DECLINE

Rasputin started his pilgrimage to Moscow, to St. Petersburg and, without fully realizing it, towards the Imperial Court of Russia. In the village of Pokrowskoje, there was concern for Anna, the cousin of pope Pjotr. She was a woman of good reputation, pious and generous, married to the merchant Dimitri. She had a son at the age of 20, but, to her regret, he was the only one. She was now nearly 50, but still young looking, thanks also to her excellent health. Anna, in the last two months, had not felt well. Her body, usually fit, looked inflated and she was not smiling anymore. The doctor came from the district of Tobolsk and his diagnosis was that Anna suffered from a malignant disease, and she could not be saved. Rasputin was informed of the situation by his wife. He went to see Anna and looked for a while at her sad face. Rasputin used to look at people using his eyes like a scalpel. Then his clear, calm and reassuring voice was heard, "Anna, do not worry, you are going to be a mother again. Be faithful to God."

The news spread rapidly throughout all the nearby districts and was received with mixed feelings. How could Anna, at her age, be a mother again? After a few months, Rasputin was proved right and everybody laughed at the Tobolsk doctor. So the reputation of Rasputin increased and spread to new villages and cities.

He was certainly not a normal individual, also from a physiological and psychological point of view. His innate hypnotic power was increased by the steadiness of his pupils. His eyes, of steel gray color, seemed capable of looking at the sun with the same easiness as at a shadow.

Rasputin never smiled. Instead he knew all the variances of the laugh, from the obscene to the sardonic, to the tragic. He possessed an innate suggestive power capable of turning away the instinctive repugnance his body was emanating. The physical appearance of Rasputin was really disturbing. He also used to dress very poorly, and modified this strange habit only during his late stay at Court. His face was often distorted in a morbid grimace, sensual and cruel. His small eyes, nearly colorless, were too close and his eyebrows too thick. A wart deformed his right eye. An irregular line divided his big head covered by uncombed hair. On his forehead was a purple scar. His skin, burned by the sun, was wrinkled, and his beard, reddish and hirsute, increased the unpleasant impression he presented. One day, as faith would have it, Grigori Rasputin, strange and biblical personality, was privileged to be invited to the Court of the Great Czars of Russia.

He was introduced by Father Teophan to Grand Duchess

Anastasia, confidant, and to dame Anna Wyrubova, personal friend of the Czarina. All were waiting for Rasputin. The presumptuous members of the nobility had already heard about the *muzhik*. They were skeptical and amused at the same time, with a morbid curiosity to see him. After all, the thaumaturgists were fashionable.

For the useless and stupid courtesans, the clairvoyant monks and fortuneteller gypsies were a delightful and amusing pastime, probably hiding a certain amount of sadism.

The Czar Nicholas II, following his father's habits, encouraged those strange individuals to frequent the Court. Nicholas II knew that Alexandra, the Czarina, was very pleased to know and listen to these people, and he wanted to please her. When Grigori Rasputin made his entrance into the elegant and luxurious halls of the Court, crowded with aristocrats, dames and high officers, nobody liked him. A murmur of displeased surprise greeted him. He entered slowly, walking in the typical manner of the poor *muzhik*. His look, his dress, and his face made a negative impression on those present. When he started to speak, the first sentences were practically incomprehensible. But he only needed a few seconds to get back his natural theatrical self-confidence. He continued to proceed slowly, under the close attention of the audience, and the tone of his voice progressively raised. The tone of his speech was grave and animated, and the more he spoke, the more it was binding. While he was speaking, his personal appearance also became authoritative and dignified. His head slightly inclined towards the left shoulder, and his small clear eyes, with blue tint, moved around restlessly, as if they were looking for something or somebody.

It certainly was this "look," restless initially and then magnetically powerful, that stopped, as by enchantment, the critical murmur reserved for Rasputin when he first entered. This strong and penetrating aspect seemed to have paralyzed the noble crowd. The magic was in his eyes, disconcerting at first, but then becoming friendly and confident. Also the voice, raucous, illiterate, and devastated by alcohol, opened wounds in the listener, but was also persuasive, grave, pleasant, and convincing.

While talking he used to turn his head to one side, like a minister in confession and then his speech was benign like his look. But suddenly, voice and look would change, and his entire body seemed like it was burning of an unbearable sensual passion, that made him tremble.

Once again, he could move away from this passionate approach to the serene and tender, shocking the listener. Rasputin was certainly a very good actor, with an intuitive instinct for the *coup de théâtre*. In these circumstances he moved his hands, usually folded on his chest, like an orchestra director, with force and elegance. The man was certainly helped by a powerful and innate force, the occult force of creating magnetism, balancing intuition with divination, polemics and leadership, charisma and wellbeing.

The Siberian *starets* had a very unique and personal attitude, in a country and at a time when aristocracy was given maximum power, and everybody, particularly the poor farmers, did not even dare to look at them in the eyes.

Rasputin never kissed the hands of aristocrats nor authorities, and he talked to them as equal to equal, with dignity and without fear. Rasputin's presentation at the Court lasted several hours and at the end he was the counselor and the friend of the Imperial family. When leaving, he saluted everybody in the same manner, without distinction of sex or social status. Solemn and enigmatic, he bent slightly and launched three kisses in the typical way of the wandering monks.

In the year 1904, the fame of Grigori Rasputin arrived in St. Petersburg. Father John of Kronstadt, known for his "visions," wanted to meet the Siberian prophet in his convent. After a long interview, he realized that Rasputin was touched by God. The Pope Ivan of Kronstadt was also a medicine man and succeeded in healing from a distance.

This was a mystery as well as a challenge for the scientific and medical world. His methods remained unknown and only Rasputin, who, by intuition, grasped them, tried to emulate him. The Dean of the theological University of St. Petersburg, prelate and confessor of the Czarina, asked Rasputin to visit him, in the hope that divine grace would have inspired that simple mind, a victim of demonic powers.

It is reported that the young and cultivated students of the

Academy had believed that Rasputin was a charlatan; but after their initial skepticism they changed their mind and admired the "responses" of the *stranniki*. He showed them how to reach sapience in other ways than books. The Dean tried another confrontation with Rasputin, who kept his eyes on him all the time, until the Dean became so confused he would speak illogically. At the end of the meeting he asked Rasputin to bless him. Then he introduced Rasputin to the Bishop Hermogene Sator, who introduced him to the monk Yliodor of Zaryzin, a famed preacher, powerful and feared. He was tall and fit, with hypnotic eyes, a sharp and acute voice, and irresistible strength. At the beginning Yliodor did not trust Rasputin, but after the first meeting, now partially convinced, he decided to introduce him to the committee of the "True Russians," an association of political reactionaries. The members of the association, as it appears from secret files subsequently disclaimed, feared the favor given by the Court to a number of charlatans, shamans, and fanatics of various sources. They agreed in a mutual complicity pact, to show friendship to Rasputin, hoping that, by controlling him, they could avoid a proliferation of personal enemies in the Court.

The grand duke Nicholas Nicolaievic, Commander in Chief of the entire Russian army was a sort of imperious giant, proud of his noble origin and ambitious for his position. He was very diffident when he first talked to Rasputin. He decided to unmask him and challenged him to heal somebody under his very eyes. The grand duke had a faithful servant, Andrej, who had suffered for several years of a hic-cough crisis that weakened him to the point of death. Rasputin prepared a mixture of medicinal herbs and deposed it on Andrej's stomach, put his right hand under his head and prayed for him. In ten minutes the hic-cough had disappeared and Andrej was completely healed. This episode made Nicholas very close to Rasputin and their friendship lasted several years. The *starets* used a similar treatment with Anna Wyrubova, who was severely wounded in a hunting accident. Thanks to Rasputin she was perfectly healed.

After many years of pilgrimage, the simple *muzhik* of Pokrowskoje finally succeeded in being accepted at the Court of

Russia, in Moscow and St. Petersburg.

Rasputin loved to visit the gypsies that used to crowd the shore of the Neva during each summer and produce shows in their colorful tents. The elegant society of St. Petersburg was fascinated by their performances. Grigori was well known and loved among the gypsy community. They were aware of his origins and respected him for his qualities as a medicine man, and understood that he was going to become a very powerful man in Russia. They also knew his inclination for women and wine.

One episode brought Rasputin into high regard among the gypsies. Once a rambling dog attacked the two twin brothers, sons of the chief of the gypsy community. The big animal was dangerously close to the boys. He was growling and menacing, his eyes red and foaming with rage. Rasputin happened to be there. He moved, slowly but resolutely towards the scene and without any other words put his hands around the neck of the beast and threw it away against the wheels of a carriage. He then immediately took the boys into a tent and prepared one of his miraculous mixtures of medicinal herbs. After having cleaned the leg wounds caused by the dog, Rasputin covered them with ointment, and started to pray. All the other gypsies joined him in his prayer so that the murmur became a rosary. The father was very concerned as he noticed the high fever in his children, and told Rasputin: "Grigori ... their forehead is burning." Rasputin, extremely pale and sweating, said, "Be faithful. Your children will survive. So wants God." And so it happened. A week after, the twin brothers were playing with the other boys.

Even at Court, Rasputin maintained his passion for dancing. Sometimes the desire to dance was so strong that he had to do it regardless of the place or the company. In the middle of a conversation, he stood up and invited one of the women in the group to sing for him one of the melancholic folk songs of his native land. He then started to dance to the rhythm of the song in a very natural and instinctive style.

It was during one of these dancing performances that three

Czar messengers arrived and asked: "In the name of the Czar, is there a person called Grigori Yefimovich known as Rasputin?"

He replied, annoyed, "Yes, I am." And the messenger said, "The Czarina is looking for you and wants to see you at once. Please come with us."

He explained that the three-year-old Czarevich was dying. He suffered from hereditary hemophilia. He had accidentally fallen, causing an internal hemorrhage, high fever and inguinal swelling. Rasputin was listening in silence and his body went through a total change from the dancing mood. He became extremely serious, and, with his body trembling, started praying. The crowd joined him and all kneeled down. When Rasputin stood up he was heard to say, "The Czarevich was dying. I prayed God for him and the crisis is over. He will survive." Then he jumped on the messenger's horse and left, taking the scared man with him.

It is the year 1907, in the Castle of Zarskoje Selo, the favorite residence of Czar Nicholas II and Czarina Alexandra of Hesse. In this castle, a place of great joy and terrible sorrow, Alexei was born the 30th of July, 1904. Every corner of the garden, every room of the building contains love's secrets, sweet memories, and painful shadows. The Czar was in love with Alexandra with a mutual affection, but their relationship was hurt by a sad situation. The beautiful Alexei was born very delicate, suffering from hemophilia. The Court's doctor could not cure him. The servants in the Court whispered that it was a divine punishment from the oppressed poor people of Russia. The Czar, a gentleman of small stature, was a very complex person. Shy and weak, he was not the right sovereign to handle a country of extreme vastness, crossed by internal social problems, dominated by a vain aristocracy inept to represent its role, but only involved in personal intrigues. Fatalist, resigned and choleric, the Czar was obsessed by the terror of misfortunes.

An atrocious "karma" was really influencing his country, hit by a series of natural and social disasters.

The Czarina was called *niemka*—"the German"—but unfairly so, as she was able to assimilate the most ancient and obscure characteristics of the Russian soul, with their subtle religious, mystical and sometimes superstitious approach. Little Alexei was suffering of hemophilia, a hereditary malady that does not forgive, a disease of the blood that loses the ability to coagulate. Hemorrhages became very frequent and difficult to control and stop. Sometimes even a small trauma, a superficial wound or a coughing attack, can provoke a violent bleeding.

During this time, Russia was troubled by several insurrections and social uprisings, and the Czar, scared and confused, renounced his authority and left full power to the Head of his Cabinet and the Grand Dukes who stifled the rebellions with blood and great cruelty.

The Czar and his wife, overcome by a profound melancholy, preferred to live in the castle of Zarskoje Selo, finding relief in religious mysticism and in the common faith in the *strannikis*. Alexei was not getting better, and all cures and treatments seemed useless. Various medicine men and thaumaturgists tried in vain to help him: Professor Philippe from France, the hysterical visionary Daria Ossipova, the disfigured and exalted Mitja with his oracle-teller and shaman Badmajeff, the French magician Papus and the famous medicine man Encausse. The Czar was born in 1868, the Czarina in 1872. The four daughters Olga in 1895, Tatjana in 1897, Maria in 1899 and Anastasia in 1901.

At about midnight of the 16th of June 1907, Rasputin entered from a small door situated at the back of the palace and was received in the Czar's private office. Present with the Czar and his wife were their four daughters, Doctor Badkin and Anna Wirobova. Rasputin's look contrasted dramatically with that of the aristocrats crowding the office.

He kissed the Czar and the Czarina and said, "Little mother, I have prayed for the Czarevich one hour ago. He is improving and will not die." The Czarina was very pale and her lips trembled. "In reality you have made a miracle, Father Grigori, one hour ago the fever disappeared and Alexei was feeling better."

Rasputin replied, "He will survive. Take me to see him now." Anna Wirobowa, the Czarina's confidant, lighted two candles in front of an icon representing Mother Mary.

Little Alexei was asleep and seemed quiet. In the dark of his bedroom the Czarina saw Rasputin kneel down and pray ardently. After a while Rasputin stood up and with his right hand touched the forehead of the boy in a mysterious sign. "Your son, little mother, is sleeping and safe. The fever is gone. He will live." Those present remarked in astonishment that the bruise caused by his fall had disappeared from his forehead. All that day he had suffered earaches, headaches and muscular pain. Two hours before he fell asleep and now was slowly waking up. Rasputin, whom he did not know initially, scared him, so Rasputin told him "No fear, Alexei, now you are fine. I have sent away all your troubles and tomorrow you will be playing again. I will teach you a lot of games."

Rasputin, when speaking to Alexei, undoubtedly used his powerful hypnotic power, but in a very confidential and friendly way. He told him about the great country Siberia and told him the old stories heard when he was a boy. There everything was different. Men were good, strong and generous, and even the animals could be understood by men.

These stories worked on the psyche of Alexei and created a feeling of wellbeing and confidence with regard to Rasputin. The magnetic "prana" was functioning. Rasputin made a great impression on the Czar and his family. They wanted him to stay with them forever. The Czar's personal diary reads on the 19th day of July 1907: "We have met a man from God, called Grigori coming from Tobolsk. His prayers have saved Alexei from a sure death." The local Cossack Derevenko was the bodyguard of Czarevich Alexei. He was strong and massive, but simple at heart and ready to give his life for the boy. Initially he did not like Rasputin, but changed his mind when he saw what he did for Alexei. For him Rasputin was the protector sent by God.

It is reported that Rasputin was involved in spiritualistic practices in St. Petersburg and that he seemed to master a natural predisposition. He had certainly followed the school and teaching of two famous Russians, Alex Aksakov and Alex Nikolajevic. The first is considered the father of metapsychic research and sponsored the Foundation of Psychic Studies in Moscow. The second gave a remarkable contribution to the development of serious psychic studies and metapsychic questions in Russia. They both died in St.

Petersburg in 1903.

SCANDALS AND INTRIGUES AT THE COURT

The destiny of the Siberian *muzhik* was now definitely marked. "The beloved friend"—this is how the Imperial family called him— had become irreplaceable. He was consulted for help and advice on projects, regulations, orders and enemies.

The gratefulness for the thaumaturgist Rasputin seemed to be without limits. In such a situation, Rasputin used all his power to attack what he considered the "fake" shamans and thaumaturgists who used to crowd the Russian Court. He did the same for the useless and corrupt bureaucrats, responsible for oppressing the people instead of serving them.

Unfortunately—but history cannot be made with "ifs" and "buts"—Rasputin probably arrived at the Court when it was already too late. The Russian situation was profoundly deteriorated, and so many people who took advantage of the moral devastation of the ruling class fought the generous effort carried out by Rasputin. The men and women who had lost confidence in the Imperial family got together to plot against Rasputin, but nobody had the courage to kill him. Among Rasputin's enemies, the most powerful and pitiless was the monk Yliodor. Rasputin had been the only one to succeed in healing Alexei and his success had humiliated Yliodor, who had had a reputation as a medicine man. He had tried, unsuccessfully, to cure the Czarevich.

In the year 1911, Rasputin began to be openly involved in Russian politics and to play a role in the power struggle of that troubled country. He was the subtle mastermind that controlled the Czar and manipulated the decision making process in internal and foreign affairs. Hiring and firing, nominations and promotions of high officials and bureaucrats, were all decided with Rasputin's involvement, very often in a temperamental and emotional manner. He had become extremely powerful. His house was always crowded and he loved to entertain. Since his arrival in Moscow his dress code had changed and now he enjoyed elegant clothes, silky black tunics and soft leather boots.

Three secretaries assisted him in handling daily correspondence and solving the less important questions: Yosif, Simonovich and Dobrowolskj. A peasant woman, Katja, loyal, incorruptible and proud, was his personal servant. She was an admirer of Rasputin, who severely reprimanded the more noisy and irreverent guests. Rasputin seemed authorized to do everything he wanted, and she loved that. She adored him when he was trying to write something with his long and bony hands. Usually the result was some unclear signs.

Rasputin, to overcome his embarrassment, used to say: "Katja, with these fingers I handle the Russian Empire." This statement was terribly true. In those days the fate of Russia was determined and guided by Rasputin, who also used to say, in reference to the Imperial couple, "The little father and the little mother are two big children. They are in bad need of guidance, and I am their guide."

In fact, the relations between Rasputin and the Imperial couple went through various stages. At the beginning they were impressed. They admired and were moved by the man who healed their son. Later they were confused, when Rasputin revealed his religious thoughts and his theatrical behavior. Even so, he always maintained a strong hold on them. Thanks to his extrovert personality, he fulfilled their empty life and was always available to assist their souls. He used to deal with them in a simple and direct style, sometimes avoiding the formal politeness they were used to being treated with.

Certainly they were impressed by this approach, which seemed to them to represent the true spirit of their country. The bizarre monk who spoke to them with an audacious familiarity, so different from the hypocrisy and adulation of the courtesans, became the symbol of the simplicity and honesty of the country people. The very people with whom they had lost contact. Rasputin's enemies, particularly among the courtesans, increased. Now also several women were to play a negative influence in his life.

One, in particular, was the famous and mysterious Elisalex. She was intimate with political personalities, had a decisive importance in Rasputin's destiny, and was linked to various scandals. Also affecting him was her friend Anna. Olga Losctina, former lover of the monk Yliodor, became Rasputin's favorite, and Nun Akulina of the convent of St. Thikon, once devil possessed but exorcised by Rasputin.

The daughters of the King of Montenegro were loyal to the *muzhik* and always present to his spiritual sessions. The numberless dames of the Court rivals in love and nicknamed *Rasputinitzky*.

But the most dangerous was Elisalex. This beautiful woman was the centerpiece of the conversation in all St. Petersburg's parties. Who was she?

The information is limited. She was born in the countryside, near Jaroslav, the daughter of a wealthy landowner who retired early in a great mansion rich with artworks collected during years of travelling all over the world. Only the Yussupov family was believed to have a richer library in their home. Elisalex was a very intelligent lady with a personality capable of manipulating people's minds. She was supposed to have unusual friends outside the Court and once was heard to say to Count Fedor, "My good friend, you know how the Russian people are indolent and dreamers. I know a person that can use this indolence and make it a powerful tool. This person is Vladimir Uljanov, called Lenin ... he is the right man for our country in these difficult times. I do trust him and I can confess you my secret, with the request of keeping it in strict confidence. I am a Bolshevik."

Elisalex had a controversial relationship with Rasputin. Once the Czarina was looking for him and the secret police found him in Elisalex's house. This gave rise to all sorts of speculations. A second episode was even stranger. One evening Rasputin was enjoying one of his "orgies" at the Yar Restaurant in Moscow. Good food, wine, dancing and gypsies. Rasputin was drunk. He talked without control about his love affairs in the Court and described in juicy detail his adventures. He went so far as to mention the Czarina, addressing her as *staraja jenscina*, an old woman, and showing a waistcoat he was wearing made by the Czarina for him.

The confidentiality of his conversation had created a certain embarrassment, but Rasputin continued freely and then started dancing with a beautiful gypsy. At the end of his dance he recognized Elisalex and furiously tore away her clothes, leaving her nearly naked on the floor. When the guests tried to stop him, he became even more enraged and rotated his belt around like a wounded beast. His friends were now disgusted and scared, and left the restaurant after paying the owner with some gold pieces for the bill and the damages. This incident created an enormous scandal and was used by Rasputin's enemies to denigrate him.

The mention of the Czarina's name in such a place was considered a sacrilege. The Chief of Police went to report these things to the Czar, but was not received. The Commander of the Imperial Residence, a good friend of Rasputin, had maneuvered to avoid it. The information on this embarrassing episode arrived at Court via indirect informants, and an official investigation was ordered. Still, Rasputin enjoyed such a good reputation that even a detailed report on that evening did not hurt him.

In fact, the Czarina declared that Rasputin (the Saint) was being tempted by the Devil and only thanks to divine assistance he saved himself. Instead, the responsibility for what happened was placed on the Devil himself, in this case Elisalex. She was forced into exile from Russia and thanks to her good contacts was able to reach Paris, were she remained.

The power of Rasputin was still very strong, but, unavoidably, his good luck was to abandon him. Some time after the accident, he was again reputed to have been involved in an event that was discussed around all of St. Petersburg. Rasputin had been invited to a top meeting with ten members of the Church in the presence of Bishop Hermogenes, including Yliodor and Mitjia. It was a plot to engage Rasputin in a furious litigation on certain questions. Bishop Hermogenes hit Rasputin with the heavy silver cross resting on his chest, as a symbol of his position. They even tried to pay him off with 500,000 rubles if he had moved away from the Imperial family. Rasputin was immovable. The Chief of Police from Kazan tried to blackmail Rasputin and told Yliodor, "Rasputin is a diabolical charlatan, depraved and lurid, and I have him in my hands." He had hoped to scare Rasputin, and threaten him with the dangers of reopening an obscure story about a rape in which Rasputin was supposed to be involved. The result was the replacement of the Chief of Police. The Home Office Cabinet Head also tried to have him killed, using hit men and former policemen. Once Rasputin was even hit by a coach and wounded.

Various interpretations had been given with regard to the magnetic force of Rasputin's eyes. He certainly was aware of his gift and made conscious and intelligent use of it. For example, it is interesting to recall the story of Semyon, a friend of Grigori, who was a witness to the Tobolsk's attempt. Informed sources reported that Yliodor, in his desire to destroy Rasputin, had promised the Mongol Boris a rich gift if he would kill Rasputin. Boris was a colossus performing in the city's squares, exhibiting force and fighting.

This is Semyon's narration: "That day I was with Grischa in Tobolsk. It was early morning and we were leaving the hospitable Natascia's house, where we had had fun with some girlfriends. Grischa was in a very good mood and we were joking. Few people were around because of the cold and the early hour. Suddenly Boris appeared, big as a giant. He was hidden and waiting to kill Rasputin. I was facing Boris, and Rasputin was in the other side. Boris took me with his unbelievable strength and literally threw me on the iced street, breaking my knees. I was screaming from pain. Rasputin had turned and was waiting for the beast to attack him. I knew that Rasputin was a robust person, but I doubted how long he could resist the attacks of the Mongol, greedy for the promised prize. Grischa avoided a punch and was fast to hit Boris on his face. That made Boris motionless for only a few seconds. This was enough time for Rasputin. He stared the colossus in the eyes in a way that seemed to go through his brain and make him defenseless. Boris tried to move his arms, but they fell down to his sides. Rasputin found the time to throw a heavy stone to his head and the Mongol collapsed on the floor. I had seen Rasputin making use of the strength of his eyes before, but never in such a fast and effective way. I really think this was a miracle and that Rasputin is protected by God."

THE END OF THE RUSSIAN EMPIRE
AND THE DEATH OF RASPUTIN

A few months before Russia entered the war the fascinating and intriguing Elisalex, along with her loyal friend Margaritha, received in her aristocratic mansion three socially disparate personalities: the French ambassador Maurice Paleologue, the British ambassador Sir George Buchanan, and the *starets* Rasputin.

Unfortunately the topics of the meeting remain unknown. Cyril and Juri, the servants of Elisalex, who served dinner that night, were subsequently invited by friends and after several libations revealed some gossip. Apparently in the meeting, top decisions regarding the entrance of Russia into war were discussed. The two Western European ambassadors were convinced that Elisalex, as a friend of Rasputin was aware of the Czar's decisions. Elisalex was playing a *double-jeux* and trying to get information both from the ambassadors and Rasputin. Cyril and Juri reported all the cunnings and tricks used by Elisalex and the ambassadors to succeed in their intent.

Rasputin, usually very talkative, spent more time listening than talking. He certainly felt the trap and his sensitive nature advised him to be careful. He was smiling at the compliments generously extended by the two important guests, and at the same time could not remove his eyes from the beautiful body of Elisalex. His brain, however, remained firm and strong. At the end of the meeting Rasputin is reported by Cyril and Juri to have said, "Certainly even the most wise men can make mistakes just as the dumbest at least once in their lives can do something of worth. As far as I am concerned I can tell you that money cannot buy the thoughts or desires of my heart."

Another episode documents that Elisalex played an important role in Rasputin's life. All of St. Petersburg was aware of the contrasts between Rasputin and Yliodor. The Count Witte, Prime Minister and personal friend of Rasputin, was trying to make peace between them because he loved Rasputin and feared Yliodor. Aware of the relationship between Rasputin and Elisalex, he intervened with the lady so that she could also help the reconciliation. An invitation to dinner was chosen as the best means to reach their goal. In attendence were Elisalex, as hostess, her friend Ljudmila, lover of Count Witte, Rasputin and Yliodor.

The dinner was proceeding very well with superb succession of *hors d'oeuvres and entrées*, accompanied by great wines. Then the conversation became more personal and Yliodor accused Rasputin of "overdoing" his healing powers in such a way that could not be accepted by a man of religion. Rasputin, touched to the quick, answered annoyed, "I am not a Saint nor a man blessed by God. Nobody can say so, as all men are sinners. I cannot heal anyone. I only pray God to do it for me."

Yliodor, with the arrival of Rasputin, had lost his reputation as the number one medicine man in town, and, worse yet, he had even lost his best client, the Czar's son. He was determined to try everything to return to the good graces of the Czar and the Imperial Family. Without discretion, he revealed his concerns and offered Rasputin a noticeable amount of money if he stopped healing Alexei. Rasputin's reply was ironic and sarcastic: "You cannot buy me. It would be like offering a comb to a Buddhist monk."

With these words dinner ended, unsuccessfully. In the meetings with the military chiefs, Rasputin was strongly opposed to the entrance of Russia into the war, and he stood as a fighter against the generals who favored it.

In this attitude Rasputin had remained the poor son of the steppe, in love with his land and opposed to all kinds of violence. Various officials, during these meetings, were to experience his angered tirades. A few months before entrance into the war, the Czar informed the Duma that Russia would not intervene in the Balkans. Evidently the wise recommendation from Rasputin had echoed in the Czar's mind and soul. The news was received bitterly by the high officials of the Army. The Grand duke Nicholas Nicolaievic immediately recognized the influence of Rasputin in the Czar's decision. The Grand Duke had been friendly with Rasputin for several years, but Rasputin's opposition to the war transformed the friendship into an implacable hate.

The Grand Duke Nicholas, in his position of Commander in Chief of all Russian armed forces, requested and obtained from the

Czar an emergency meeting. Present were the Czar, Rasputin, the Foreign Minister Sazonov, the Home Office Minister Geremykine and the War Minister Suokhomlinov. The Grand Duke spoke at length outlining the advantages deriving to Russia from a prompt intervention in the Balkans. Only the Czar, supported by Rasputin, was against intervention. The meeting rapidly became a violent collision of ideas and personalities. At one point the Grand Duke addressed Rasputin shouting in his face: "Grigori Yefimovich, you are very ungrateful. Without Anastasia and me you would still be nobody, a miserable wanderer. Turkey is our enemy. This intervention is required for the good of Russia."

Rasputin had difficulty controlling himself, but succeeded in answering moderately: "God told us not to kill, and you are asking me to disobey him. Do not forget what I am telling you ... Do you know what a battlefield resembles? The killing of pigs at midnight." Finally the Czar intervened to avoid the worst. It was not easy. Fortunately a period of calm followed. Rasputin returned to his inspired tone, his head leaning to one side, his voice back to normal. He spoke to the Czar: "Little father, the noblemen and the farmers are often fighting, because each one ignores the life of the other. They both discuss things they don't know about. Please forgive us, little father."

After that controversial meeting his friends noticed that Rasputin's mood was changing and he seemed tormented by an unnatural nervousness. Contrary to his habits, he would sit silently, eyes fixed on emptiness, for a long time. Evidently the *starets* was beginning to realize that "something" was more powerful than his magnetic force in regard to the Czar's attitude in the war issue. His exceptional extrasensory perceptions did not fail. Russia was entering the war.

The Russian people, because of his openness and generosity, loved Rasputin. He was often seen receiving important amounts of money for rendered services, and then distributing them to the needy and those asking for help. He was particularly generous with the gypsies, whose songs he was fond of. He also never forgot his wife and children, and regularly sent money to them.

In St. Petersburg the dirty story of Kazan was told many, many times. In that town one evening, five thugs armed with knives and sticks attacked Rasputin to kill him. The strong Siberian did not lose his head. He broke the only light in the street and threw himself in the fight. He was able to get two of them by the head and crushed them together. The other three got scared and ran away. The Ochrana police agents were replaced, the Head of Police was sent to Siberia and the Bishop Hermogenes exiled to a Lithuanian monastery. By the end of 1911 Rasputin traveled to Constantinople. He was fed up with the calumnies and the attacks of which he had been the victim. When he was away the crisis of Alexei became more frequent and he received a cablegram from the Czarina: "Father Grigori, I cannot stand your absence for any longer. My life is sad and empty without you, my consoler and master. Alexei has had a new relapse. Do not worry for Kokotzeff, he will get what he deserves. Forgive me if I doubted. Please come back for me and for Alexei's life." Rasputin's answer to the Czarina was not late: "God has listened to your prayers and your tears. Do not be sad, your son will survive, provided the doctors stop tormenting him." The Empress showed the cablegram to the Czar and he sent the doctors away. Immediately the son's condition improved and the fever disappeared. Nobody could give a scientific explanation for this; it was probably another miracle.

On that occasion the Czar said to the Court, "The defamers of Rasputin are idiots. I know him well." After Rasputin returned, he was again offered money by Kokotzeff (this time 300,000 rubles) to leave Court. An indignant Rasputin replied, "You should have learned by now that I cannot be bought. I only obey God's voice and no force on earth can make me do things against his orders." Rasputin was aware that the people from his country, the farmers, the *muzhiks* of Russia, stood on his side. He did a lot for them. He particularly tried, with all his power, to avoid war, because this would have meant the killing of a great number of these people, these farmers, these *muzhiks*. Grigori said to the Generals, "War offends God, and insults the people." In May 1914 Rasputin went back to Siberia. They did not listen to his advice and Russia entered war. The 29th day of June 1914 was a terrible date for the

Imperial family. The envious and vindictive monk Yliodor partially succeeded in the plan that tormented him for years. Kionja, one of his disciples, a violent and bigoted woman, was able to hit Rasputin in the stomach with a sharpened knife, while pretending to present a petition. Then she ran away screaming that she killed the Devil.

Rasputin was not ready to die and recovered after several days in the hospital. Yliodor disappeared into a foreign country and Kionja ended in Siberia. Grigori forgave them, but Yliodor continued to plot against Rasputin to obtain the "vendetta" which was now so close. The 31st day of July 1914 the Czar, influenced by the Generals and not listening to Rasputin, decide to declare war against Germany. General mobilization took place. In September, Rasputin returned to St. Petersburg and was seen to be silent, immersed in tragic thoughts. The Czar was pleased with the initial positive news from the war front. Rasputin asked him, "Little Father, how many Russians have died so far?" The Czar admitted that it was a remarkable number, but that the Austrians suffered an even higher death toll. Rasputin then said, "They are all sons of God, and these figures make me very sad. Even if we are doing well from a military point of view, I am afraid that the social situation is going to change." Stubbornly, Rasputin continued his fight against the war.

Many things were rapidly changing. Many high officials disappeared. In 1916 he was able to entertain secret negotiations in Stockholm to sign a separate peace treaty with Germany, but was accused of treason by a group of aristocrats. The Home Office Minister, Protopopov, and Prime Minister Strumer were also accused of being secret agents in the service of Germany, because they were friends of Rasputin.

In this particularly tragic situation the plots and the maneuvers for power increased and went out of control. In 1916, during the course of the war, an insurrection against the Czar developed in Central Asia. The repression, as usual, was fast and cruel, and several poor farmers were killed. Among the military powers, a rumor started that Rasputin told the Czar that Russia would have lost the war if they had sent the "second class" of Army (the one the Czar's son belonged to) to the front. This was untrue. What really happened was that in 1914, at the beginning of the war, the majority of soldiers came from the farms. They had been literally taken by force from their lands, with the threat of being court martialled if they refused. Consequently the troop's morale was very low, and the lack of motivation was not conducive to battle. Because of his political intrigues, Rasputin lost the friendship of the most powerful people in the Court. Among them Prince Yusupov, the Grand Duke Dimitri Pavlovic, a member of the Duma Purishko.

They were the plotters that, in order to avoid a catastrophe and probably also to keep their prestige in the Court, organized Rasputin's assassination. It was a useless murder, because the tragedy that was overtaking Russia could not be stopped. The many prophecies of Rasputin were truthful and his words to the Czarina sounded like a premonition: "If you separate from me, in less than six months you will lose throne and life. I have terrible nightmares and through them I see my future. I will die very soon, amidst terrible suffering, and you, little mother, will lose your crown and will be massacred with the rest of your family." Rasputin's enemies were looking for the killers who could remove the unwanted *starets*. They found them not among the poor farmers, who were Rasputin's allies, but in the vain and useless relatives of the Czar.

The "execution" committee was composed of five members: the Grand Duke Dimitr; Prince Felix Yusupov, the pale artist with a morbid soul; the Duma member Purishkovich, the military surgeon; the lieutenant Suchotin; and the Polish Doctor Lasovert, the Yusupov family's medical doctor. Grand Duke Nicholas stayed prudently covered behind the scenes. The Yusupov family was one of the richest of Russia. Felix married Grand Duchess Irina, the Czar's niece.

The prince had a feminine soprano voice and loved to play the guitar and dress in extravagant disguise. He did not enjoy a good reputation, and Rasputin used to call him "the little weak sinner." Anna Wyrubova, who knew him very well, advised Rasputin to stay away from him: "Felix is a coward, a braggart, a vile traitor in search of unusual sensations." Once in a St. Petersburg theatre he played a soprano role, dressed like a woman, and nobody, not even the director, realized it. "He likes to dress as a woman so he can attract the attention of men." Yusupov's father considered his son to be a *canaille* (a French word for proletarian) and thought that his place was in Siberia among the convicts.

Rasputin, talking to the State minister Chwostoff and his vice minister Beletzki, confided to them, "It is true that the little father and the little mother do what I want. It is true that I am the Government of Russia. But after my death the Czar will lose his crown and all of Russia will change radically."

In the meantime the political situation had become even more serious. The enemy had invaded Poland, the Russian army was disorganized and was resisting only thanks to its superior number, thanks to the bastion of its human bodies. Romania was occupied by Austrian troops. At home the revolution fomented. Although still underground, a movement of rebellion was pervading all social classes and was already evident in the largest cities like Moscow. Russia's entry into the war had surprised and exasperated Lenin. Surprised because he had incorrectly believed that all European socialist parties would have opposed war. Indignation because he, like Rasputin, considered war a manifestation of economic imperialism and therefore against the proletariat's interest. He took advantage of the situation and had the ability to transform the "imperialistic war" into the "socialist revolution." The Russian people, armed by the bourgeoisie to protect the capitalistic power, must fight against them to gain the leadership. Lenin became more optimistic with the war's development. He understood that Russia would have been in such difficulties as to provoke an uprising of the people against its government. He was right. He took all possible advantages from the war and from Germany, which had an interest in helping the enemies of the Russian power and army; i.e. the Russian Bolsheviks. The well-known Doctor Parvus, a German-Russian socialist, author of economic analysis, worked for a while for the Bolshevik party and then in the service of Germany. A good organizer and theoretician, he was a friend of Lenin and helped him to travel through Germany in 1917 and reach St. Petersburg without being stopped by the German authorities. It is said that Lenin and Parvus maintained written communications with Rasputin in the hope of organizing the transformation from a capitalistic war to a war of the classes. In reality there is no evidence of such contacts.

The plot against Rasputin continued its development. The young Felix met Grigori in the house of mutual friends, Jlona and Olga. The handsome and feminine prince was singing a delicate song and Rasputin was fascinated by the music and the gypsy guitar. This time Rasputin's instinct and intuition failed. He did not realize that such an elegant and refined young person could be a vile traitor. Felix felt that Rasputin liked him and took advantage of it. Grigori called him "his little young friend," and Felix for many months continued to lie and pretend that Rasputin was his friend. The pressuring of Yliodor set the final date. It was the 16th day of December 1916, according to the Russian calendar, the 30th according to the Gregorian calendar.

Rasputin, in his home at 68 Gorokowaia Street, was waiting in the late afternoon for his friend Felix Yusupov. Felix was going to take the *starets* to his palace at number 94 along the Moika. Felix told Rasputin that he was to meet his beautiful wife Irina, who was really in Krimea. The loyal Katja with Matrjona, the elder daughter of Rasputin, had prepared the greensilk tunic, embroidered with drawings representing dragons in red and black. The shining smooth boots and the black galoshes (the dress code now loved by Rasputin). Everything was ready when the new Home Office Minister arrived, out of breath and extremely worried, to tell him that there were rumors that his life was in danger. Grigori was not worried and told him to go back to his office. In addition his secretary, Simanovic, informed Grigori that he was in danger, but Rasputin replied, "We will see who is the strongest." At 10.15 p.m. Felix arrived, wearing a smart fur. He kissed Rasputin, who told him, "My dear little friend, is this the kiss of Judah?" and Rasputin's eyes looked very firmly at Felix's. "I have just spoken to Protopopov, who advised me not to leave home. Apparently somebody is trying to kill me, and if you want I can give you the details." Yusupov remained speechless and extremely pale. Rasputin abruptly said, "Let's go, I am ready." Katja for the first time insisted that Rasputin stay. She had intuitively felt the danger. Rasputin was again very relaxed and calm, and kissed her and his daughter. This was very unusual and Katja's eyes were full of tears. Once in the Yusupov's mansion Rasputin was accommodated in a nicely furnished secluded area. From the window one could see the main salon of the palace, always crowded with important guests.

That evening the lights were on and the orchestra was playing. Everything was fake, the music and the noise of the guests. Rasputin asked who was in the palace and Felix replied, "These are my wife's friends. They will leave shortly." Rasputin was served Krimea wine and French champagne, *hors d'oeuvres* and *canapés*.

Beautiful fresh flowers decorated the room. The food was poisoned and the wine drugged. The poison and drug came from the hospital doctor, Obukoff, friend of Prince Felix. There was enough cyanide to kill ten men. But Grigori looked fine, and Felix was nervous. "Father Grigori, how do you feel?" he asked. Rasputin replied, "My mouth has a bitter flavor. Give me more wine." Rasputin drunk and ate voraciously, and then asked Felix to play the guitar for him. Felix was singing an old folk song and Grigori seemed absent. His behavior was unnatural, as he was usually very attentive. He looked as if distracted with a sort of vacant air. Was he listening to Felix, or to his internal premonitions? Certainly he was troubled and probably his magnetic power started to weaken. He was feeling a sense of fatigue, while he continued to drink that wine and eat that food.

Now the noise from the palace had stopped, but nothing was happening. Why? *Why?* Felix was wondering, shaken and scared. That poison should have finished Rasputin by now. At 2.30 a.m., Felix, now extremely nervous, heard noises coming from upstairs. Evidently his allies in the plot were becoming nervous too. So he asked Rasputin again, "Don't you feel well Grigori?" Rasputin poured some more wine and said with great fatigue, "My head is a little heavy and my stomach upset." That's all.

How could he be behaving like nothing happened? The poison mixed in the food and in the wine was enough to kill at least ten people. Yet Grigori was not showing any signs of poisoning, only a certain melancholy. Now Grigori started to look at Felix while he continued to drink very slowly his wine; it was an enigmatic look capable of destroying Felix's nerves. The time passed, and still nothing happened. Felix was feeling very tired and could not sing anymore. Only his fingers were caressing the guitar's strings. Then suddenly he said, "Look, Grigori, look at this beautiful Christ made in ivory, a work of the Italian Renaissance." Rasputin fixed stupefied on the artwork that the young man, with trembling hands, was showing him. His face now took on an expression of serenity and happiness. A few more minutes and the gun, this was in fact the Renaissance artwork, shot once, twice, three times. Rasputin's body fell on the floor, without a noise, contorting on the carpet. The young executioner, pale and trembling, was now looking at his victim. The great *starets* was at his feet, but Rasputin was not yet dead.

His eyes were changing color and took on a green light. The pain deformed his mouth, teeth closed, and blood, nearly black, and flowed out from a large wound in the left temple. Felix was fascinated by that glass-like look; those eyes that used to terrify him like a knife entering his brain, were now attracting him with even more power and terror. It was impossible to resist. and Felix, moved by an hypnotic force coming from Rasputin eyes, was obliged to kneel down to his body in a way that seemed a manifestation of respect. It was a question of seconds, and Rasputin's hands, like fangs, held his neck to strangle him. Felix screamed harshly, awakened from his half-hypnotic state and jumped back, crazed by terror. He took a heavy stick covered with iron and savagely hit several times the lifeless body of Rasputin. Felix's servant, who returned to the scene when he heard the noise, witnessed the terrible outburst and the useless ferocity.

After a while the plotters met in the room realizing that, finally, the attempt to kill Rasputin had succeeded. To divert the policemen of the Ochrana, Dimitri and Lasovert put Rasputin's garments on lieutenant Suchotin and went by car to the *starets'* house. Yusupov stayed with Putishkovich in the room with the body. After all, the devil might still be alive. The representative of the Duma moved close to Rasputin's body and shook it. To his astonishment the left eyelid started to shrink spasmodically. His eyes opened and a greenish light glimmered in the dark of the room. The two men had a terrible and obsessive feeling. Rasputin was again able to move. On all fours he reached the stairs and the door looking into the garden. With his remaining strength he opened the door, pulling it desperately. Purishkovich followed him and shot three more times. A policeman called from the outside, "Your excellence, we heard a shooting," and Felix responded quickly, "Don't worry, it is nothing. One of my guests is just shooting in the air." Rasputin's body was brought back into the room, and covered with a blanket. After a while the Grand Duke's car returned, bringing also the lieutenant and the doctor. They load up the body, folding its legs and arms, and went in the direction of the Petroski Bridge on the Neva. The body of Rasputin was thrown into the icy waters.

One of Rasputin's black galoshes was found on the bridge. After a long and distressed search, the disfigured body of the *starets* was recovered from the river. The body could not reach the Gulf of Finland, as hoped by the killers, since the glacier did block it. The skull was smashed, the right eye came out and was swinging attached only by a ligament. A quantity of water was found in the stomach, and one hand was freed from the ropes, indicating that Rasputin, still alive when he was thrown in the river, had desperately tried to save himself.

The funeral of the *starets*, at State's expense and with official protocol, took place the 21st day of December. The Court ordered a day of mourning. Father Teophan celebrated the last services and the burial was in the park of Zarskoje Selo. The Imperial family attended the ceremony, according to the rituals of the Orthodox Church. The Czarina deposited a sacred image in the tomb of Rasputin. On the back she wrote, "My loved and sublime martyr, please give me your blessing so that I can be escorted by you for the remainder of my sad life on Earth. Remember us in your prayers from Heaven. Alexandra." The State Police investigated and discovered the truth, but the power of the families Yussupov and Dimitri was a great deterrent to justice. The participation in the murder of two such important members of the noble class created embarrassment to the Ochrana, made the investigation very awkward and gave strength to the plotters. The Czarina used to say that Rasputin was the intermediary between her, the Czar and God. But in this occasion she could not influence her husband who, threatened also by the difficult political and social situation, did not find the strength to obtain justice. The plotters received a mild and short exile in their rich summer residences. After a certain time, the Czar finally had the courage to condemn the murder, at least with words: "I, Nicholas the Second, am ashamed to face Great Russia for the murder of Grigori Rasputin, caused by the hands of people belonging to my family."

But history moved on, and the prophecies of Rasputin became inexorably true. "When I will not be here to protect you, you will lose your son, your throne, your life. But even worse will be my enemies' fate. I know that I will die among terrible pain, but, even if the wind tries to disperse my ashes, I will still do miracles from the tomb. Thanks to my prayers, sick people will recover and sterile women will birth children." This, at least in part, was true. The mourning for Rasputin's death was not yet over, and his enemy Yliodor, not satisfied with Rasputin's death, was still plotting to throw mud on his memory. He continued to maneuver to have bad press and gossiping to darken Rasputin's image. This only succeeded in increasing the already tense situation in Russia. On the night of the 22nd day of March 1917, the same day that the Czar abdicated, a group of drunken soldiers profaned Rasputin's tomb, devastated the sepulchre and removed Rasputin's corpse to take it to the forest of Pargalowo. There other soldiers built a funeral pyre. Rasputin's corpse, already half-putrefied, was covered with petroleum and cremated high on the funeral pyre. The fire lasted more than six hours until dawn. Hundreds of *muzhiks*, arriving from the nearer lands, witnessed in awe this macabre ceremony, so similar to the witch's sacrifices of the Inquisition.

Here was the man, the *muzhik*, the *starets*. Here was the friend of the Czar and the Czarina, sent by God, who had healed the sick, who had helped the poor, who always had had a word of love for those in need.

When the soldiers buried the ashes under the snow, those hundreds of peasants cross themselves in respect for the man that came from their land and was one of them, a son of the land where they were born, suffered, and where they would for many years to come.

On the 13th day of August 1917, the Imperial family was directed, by the forces of history, to the district of Tobolsk in Siberia, the birthplace of Rasputin. Little Alexei, the innocent friend of the *starets*, was happy because he hoped he would finally meet some of those fascinating personalities Rasputin told him about. Maybe he would also succeed in talking to the animals, the horses that were the best friends of his friend Grigori. Nicholas Romanov and Alexandra of Assia were headed towards the end of their lives. In vain they hoped to see in the vaste steppe the image of the man that helped them so many times in the past. The Imperial family was chained and imprisoned to wait for the execution on the 16th of July 1918. Their prison was a poor house in Ekaterinburh, a small city not far away from Rasputin's birthplace. So the prophecies of Rasputin were becoming fulfilled.

Rasputin had three children: Dimitri, who was tragically and mysteriously killed; Varvara, the daughter who died by starvation together with her mother; and Maria the second daughter, still alive *(Note: at the time this book was originally written, in 1960)*. Maria is in possession of the spiritual will of her father. It says, "My beloved, a tragedy is coming. The face of Our Saint Mother is darkened. Her spirit is troubled. The divine rage is going to be terrible. Where can I hide? It is written: be awake, as you don't know the hour or the day. There will be blood and tears. I know that my life is ending. God knows the way of our sufferance. The deaths are going to be thousands and thousands. Brother will kill brother. The earth will shake. Famine and plague will arrive. Pray for your salvation. Thanks to Our Savior and to his Mother. Grigori."

To complete the narration of Rasputin's life it is of interest to return to a woman who was important in his destiny: Elisalex. In a document she wrote on Rasputin she said: "Grigori had a strong prophetic gift, but this did not make him happy at all. All his prophecies had something tragic: the destiny of the Imperial family, the war, the revolution. I had been a *Rasputinitzky* and I don't regret that. In his eyes shone a special light, called by his admirers 'religious fervor.' He had an extraordinary physical strength. He was violent and brutal, but also kind and soft. He was a religious satyr, I a pagan nymph. The two extremes touch each other. My story is also the story of Russia. I will be described as liberated woman, which is probably true. But they will have to report also that all important decisions regarding Russia were decided first by Rasputin and my friends in my home. Then they were passed to the Czarina who officially approved them. Rasputin had a great power over the Imperial family, but I was behind him. I will never forget Rasputin's eyes. They were like the windows of his soul, and from those windows one could see his entire world. The vast land of his country, the flowers of the tundra, the shining of the winter snow, the splendor of nature and the eternal seduction of the flesh and of carnal love."

Many books, articles, and even movies have told the history of Rasputin. He has been described in many different ways: an impostor, a charlatan, a drunkard, a saint. In the history of "divination" we often find controversial personalities were good and bad, often taken to extremes, all mixed together. We believe that in the "Oracle" Rasputin has given us the best part of his personality. The rest belongs to one of the more complex periods of European History.

HOW TO USE
THE ORACLE OF RASPUTIN

1. Keep diligently the three Talismans/Amulets. Do not fold them. Do not write on them.
2. The relation between the user and the Oracle is "personal and confidential."
3. Look at the Questions listed at the pages 63-66 of the Oracle and choose the one you are really interested in.
4. Shuffle the three Talismans/Amulets without looking at them. Repeat mentally, with your eyes closed, your question for at least nine times. This is a simple operation, but requires concentration.
5. After you have repeated the question for at least nine times, draw one Talisman/Amulet and take note of the "element" represented in the Talisman/Amulet (AIR—FIRE—WATER).
6. Put back the Talisman/Amulet with the other two and repeat the operation two more times exactly in the same way. The result will be a combination of the three elements (i.e. AIR—AIR—FIRE or FIRE —WATER—AIR, and so on). There are 27 possible combinations.
7. Read in the Table of Responses on the page corresponding to the required question, the response of the Oracle appearing under the chosen combination.
8. For example, if the chosen combination is AIR—FIRE—WATER the correct response will appear in the same order AIR—FIRE— WATER on the list of the responses.
9. Keep in mind that all questions are numbered and the responses are reported under the same number.
10. The first response is the correct one. If the response is repeated twice on the same day it is always the first response that counts.
11. Given the particular nature of the Oracle, and in view to obtain serious and pertinent responses, it is advisable not to use the Oracle as a game and to ask appropriate questions.

TABLE OF QUESTIONS

1. What will be the duration of my life on Earth?

2. Which job or profession should I undertake?

3. Am I going to be successful in life?

4. Am I going to have my own family?

5. Am I going to get married with the person I love, and when?

6. Is my marriage going to be happy?

7. Are my financial struggles going to be over?

8. Is the voyage I am taking going to meet favorable results?

9. Are my moral struggles going to be over?

10. Can my physical illness be cured?

11. Does my dream bring good auspices?

12. Is my presentiment going to become reality?

13. Will the ill person I am thinking of going to be restored?

14. What will be the result of my legal issue?

15. What will be the result of my project?

16.   Are my misfortunes going to end?

17.   Is the person I am living together with going to be always faithful?

18.   Is my life going to be financially prosperous?

19.   Am I going to have children and will they bring joy to me?

20.   Do I have loyal and generous friends?

21.   Am I lucky in gambling?

22.   Will I travel extensively in the near future?

23.   Does the person I love correspond to me?

24.   Will I inherit real estate properties?

25.   Do I have many enemies and are they dangerous?

26.   Will I be able to retire one day in good financial conditions?

27.   Is my reputation enjoying esteem and trust?

28.   What is the near future bringing to me?

29.   Is the person who is far away thinking about me and coming back?

30.   How is my name and my works going to be judged by the posterity?

31.   Will I witness political or military changes?

32.   Will I marry the "ideal?"

33. Am I going to be lucky in love?

34. Will I move to a foreign country?

35. Are my descendants going to be happy after my death, and will they remember me?

36. Is my life going to be bustling?

37. Are calumnies against my person going to damage my career and life?

38. Will I receive important communication, and what will be the content?

39. What will be the consequences of the damage I have suffered?

40. Will I have to fight with a rival?

41. Will I be happy after the changes in my present situation?

42. Is the person I am thinking about going to be helpful?

43. Will I keep my present position?

44. Is the person I am thinking about going to be fortunate?

45. What is my true character?

46. What will be the result of the speculative transaction I have planned?

47. What is the true character of the person I am thinking of?

48. Will I be successful in a sport or entertainment career?

49.   Is the person I am dealing with really sincere?

50.   How will my affair end?

51.   What will be the result of my education?

52.   Is my behavior wise and honest?

53.   Will I be able to find the financial help I need?

54.   Will I be free of the person I am thinking of?

55.   Do my relatives love me, and are they sincere?

56.   Will I see improvements and/or promotions in my career?

57.   Should I change my job or business?

58.   Is my political and religious creed fair and correct?

59.   What do my parents think of me?

60.   Should I divorce?

61.   Is the person in my love affair in love with me?

62.   What will my life be like when I retire?

63.   How will my gay friendship develop?

TABLE OF RESPONSES

RESPONSES TO QUESTION #1

What will be the duration of my life on Earth?

FIRE FIRE FIRE	It could really be long. Unfortunately your way of life is making it short.
FIRE FIRE WATER	Do not waste the time Destiny gave you and your life will be long enough.
FIRE FIRE AIR	Smile at your friend and don't be afraid of your enemy. This will make your life longer.
FIRE WATER FIRE	Be more careful with the precious gift of health, and do not worry.
FIRE WATER WATER	Look out for the deadly poisons of hate and envy. They can take away many years of your life.
FIRE WATER AIR	Notwithstanding your illness, you will reach advanced seniority.
FIRE AIR FIRE	Hurry up, but still several achievements will remain to be completed.
FIRE AIR WATER	Do not worry, you can give a large part, for good deeds.
FIRE AIR AIR	You have a powerful enemy that is measuring your existence: your character.
WATER FIRE FIRE	It will be long, but not long enough to satisfy you.

WATER FIRE WATER	An excellent marriage and good friends. This is the recipe for a long life.
WATER FIRE AIR	Control your vices and you will certainly gain several years.
WATER WATER FIRE	You have the key of your vital machinery. Make a good use of it.
WATER WATER WATER	Very long, so long that you will find it boring.
WATER WATER AIR	Brief or long, your life on earth is not important. It is the next one that counts.
WATER AIR FIRE	You act too precariously. This will eventually be fatal.
WATER AIR WATER	Do not be too afraid of the end of your life. At that time many other spirits will be with you.
WATER AIR AIR	Check more carefully your health and you will enjoy it.
AIR FIRE FIRE	Why do you bother? This is the only Law really equal to all.
AIR FIRE WATER	You are taking too many risks. Be wiser and this will help you.
AIR FIRE AIR	Your life will be long, but your happiness too short.
AIR WATER FIRE	Do not have too many worries. That day you will have nothing to regret.
AIR WATER WATER	Your voyage is already expected in the world of the trespassed spirits. But they can wait.
AIR WATER AIR	You travel too fast. One day a fatal crash will be the end.
AIR AIR FIRE	Listen to my suggestion: change your lifestyle, if you want to see your descendants.
AIR AIR WATER	Look at human progress and your

AIR AIR AIR existence will be greatly improved. Short, too short. And you will not even realize it.

RESPONSES TO QUESTION #2

Which job or profession should I undertake?

FIRE FIRE FIRE Your nature is inclined to the *dolce far niente*, the sweet do nothing.

FIRE FIRE WATER Your ambitions are damaging you, and you will have to accept a normal mediocrity

FIRE FIRE AIR Your nature is "domestic"— do something related to the "house."

FIRE WATER FIRE You are delicate and sweet like honey. Do not try the medical profession.

FIRE WATER WATER Have you ever thought about the "ant?" Meditate and act accordingly.

FIRE WATER AIR You can become a successful farmer. In other jobs you will be mediocre.

FIRE AIR FIRE Aim at your secret dream—destiny will be good to you.

FIRE AIR WATER You do well in manipulating the truth—try politics or diplomacy.

FIRE AIR AIR You are like the wind of the Siberian steppe—your nature is impetuous and changeable.

WATER FIRE FIRE You are a very pragmatic person who does not like complicated theories. Keep this in mind and you will be successful.

WATER FIRE WATER You are very hesitant and I want to

	give you advice—try small enterprise.
WATER FIRE AIR	You are a good strategist and a shrewd sophist. Go ahead in politics or law.
WATER WATER FIRE	Follow the road where you have to be more astute than intelligent.
WATER WATER WATER	Don't ask for advice. I know that you will follow your instinct.
WATER WATER AIR	You are good at planning, not in implementing. Others will have to do the work for you.
WATER AIR FIRE	You have no problem in changing your opinions. Politics is a good try.
WATER AIR WATER	Choose a task that does not require too much physical effort. Don't rely too much on your health.
WATER AIR AIR	Any job where you have to travel a great deal.
AIR FIRE FIRE	In your stars it is written: "Come to terms with yourself, and you will be happy."
AIR FIRE WATER	You have a sensitive and responsive nature—occultism and/or psychology can be a good choice.
AIR FIRE AIR	Your aim is to become a College professor, but your soul will always be restless and unsatisfied.
AIR WATER FIRE	You could follow the road of gambling, but beware—one day your luck will abandon you.
AIR WATER WATER	You like to appear as an atheist, but your soul is very religious, and you could make a great Minister of God.
AIR WATER AIR	Why do you ask? Many moons will pass and you will continue to ask.
AIR AIR FIRE	Do not worry too much. Your

nature is very accommodating, and you will always find a way to live your life.

AIR AIR WATER   You have talent and a certain genius. Try entertainment or the fine arts.

AIR AIR AIR   Your inclination may lead to different roads, but no one is going to be the perfect one.

RESPONSES TO QUESTION #3

Am I going to be successful in life?

FIRE FIRE FIRE   You will, provided you focus on improving your determination and your character's flexibility.

FIRE FIRE WATER   If you attempt the project you have in mind, you may meet your goals faster than you think

FIRE FIRE AIR   Follow the current and avoid the vortexes, and you will make it.

FIRE WATER FIRE   You will succeed, but you will have to go abroad to another country.

FIRE WATER WATER   Yes, you will. But this will not warm up your icy spirit.

FIRE WATER AIR   The second half of your life will be much better than the first.

FIRE AIR FIRE   Your success is written in the stars—and this is thanks to your well balanced nature

FIRE AIR WATER   Your success reminds me of the fish. Look at the fisherman and the success will be yours.

FIRE AIR AIR   Insist and persist with

	determination and strength. The goal is not too far away.
WATER FIRE FIRE	You will be successful—rapidly and satisfactorily—if you make well balanced use of the qualities of your heart and of your mind.
WATER FIRE WATER	The reaching of your success is in line with your means.
WATER FIRE AIR	The goal you are looking for will be - unfortunately—missed at the very last moment.
WATER WATER FIRE	Be tenacious in your great fight. You will receive the prize you deserve.
WATER WATER WATER	Certainly—but very late. You will have to fight and struggle in the hard way.
WATER WATER AIR	Yes, when your back has learned the art of bowing.
WATER AIR FIRE	You will succeed, but you will have to walk over one who once helped you.
WATER AIR WATER	Your nature is too timorous. Change it, or you will not change your destiny.
WATER AIR AIR	Your success is like the astute fox— but you have a very good dog: your luck.
AIR FIRE FIRE	The person that you love will not only give you passion, but also the decisive push in your life.
AIR FIRE WATER	You success is sure—you are very well protected.
AIR FIRE AIR	You will catch it, and it will fly away. You will catch it again, and again it will fly away.
AIR WATER FIRE	You will find many difficulties and

obstacles, but also many friendly hands.

AIR WATER WATER It is sad to be successful when your hair turns gray and your pace is fatigued.

AIR WATER AIR Be strong and aggressive and you will make it. Do not be mean to the poor and simple people.

AIR AIR FIRE You will make your goal—at last. But only after many efforts and struggles.

AIR AIR WATER You will certainly make it, thanks to your cleverness and your important supporters

AIR AIR AIR Your stars are unpropitious—but do not despair.

RESPONSES TO QUESTION #4

Am I going to have my own family?

FIRE FIRE FIRE You have the financial means, although your nature is not inclined to sacrifice.

FIRE FIRE WATER You always had it. Why are you waiting to take the final decision?

FIRE FIRE AIR You will certainly have it. But remember: the winter is long, and the firewood may not last.

FIRE WATER FIRE The answer is no—but you will still try to.

FIRE WATER WATER Yes, and your family will be good and happy.

FIRE WATER AIR Yes, but I suggest you not to do it. Your shoulders are not so strong

	and will not handle the weight.
FIRE AIR FIRE	Yes, but change your plans. You are going through a reversal.
FIRE AIR WATER	No, undoubtedly. But the Divine Providence will help you anyway.
FIRE AIR AIR	Yes, but wait as long as you can, and you will not repent it.
WATER FIRE FIRE	No, but try it anyway. Your good star will help you and assist you.
WATER FIRE WATER	You will not have the financial means, but your family will provide them.
WATER FIRE AIR	The financial means are not enough. Do you believe that your nature is suitable for this step?
WATER WATER FIRE	Shortly you will have the financial means to do it. Later you will find out that they are not enough.
WATER WATER WATER	Very late in your life you will have the means, but your family will not grow.
WATER WATER AIR	Yes, and many people will be envious for your benign destiny.
WATER AIR FIRE	Yes, you can and will have your own family. The difficult task will be to keep it together.
WATER AIR WATER	Yes, but you are not strong enough to protect your family in the tougher times.
WATER AIR AIR	Be just a little more patient, as haste is very dangerous for you.
AIR FIRE FIRE	Yes, but why are you in such a hurry? Don't you prefer freedom?
AIR FIRE WATER	The answer of the stars is negative. But they don't tell me why.
AIR FIRE AIR	Yes, but be prudent. Snow melts rapidly under the sun.

AIR WATER FIRE	Look at yourself in the mirror—money is not everything.
AIR WATER WATER	Wait. You are so young, and life so beautiful.
AIR WATER AIR	You will succeed in creating your family. Watch for whom will try to destroy it.
AIR AIR FIRE	Think well and analyze the person you have chosen—my response is negative.
AIR AIR WATER	Yes, and it is understood that you will have to bear all the consequences and the natural surprises.
AIR AIR AIR	The possibility is scarce and insufficient to give you the happiness you are looking for.

RESPONSES TO QUESTION #5

Am I going to get married with the person I love, and when?

FIRE FIRE FIRE	You will have to wait a short while and you'll make a great and happy couple
FIRE FIRE WATER	Be patient for a little more time. You are certainly going to marry this person.
FIRE FIRE AIR	Move fast; otherwise you will lose the person you love, and the suffering will be unbearable.
FIRE WATER FIRE	Do not be hasty. Analyze instead attentively the character of the person you have in mind.
FIRE WATER WATER	The person you desire is not

	suitable for marriage. Slow down.
FIRE WATER AIR	The time is far away—but it will arrive
FIRE AIR FIRE	Waiting will be long and troubled— you have a strong rival.
FIRE AIR WATER	This marriage will be delayed because of obstacles and you will finally marry another person.
FIRE AIR AIR	You will marry this person very soon, notwithstanding the many obstacles.
WATER FIRE FIRE	No. The stars are on your side, and will protect you.
WATER FIRE WATER	Not so soon. For the time being continue to stay together.
WATER FIRE AIR	You will marry soon enough, but not with the person you are thinking.
WATER WATER FIRE	No, you will not succeed. Suddenly another person will appear.
WATER WATER WATER	No, it is not possible. Do not force your Destiny.
WATER WATER AIR	No. Unexpected and decisive conditions will make it impossible.
WATER AIR FIRE	Yes—soon. But this person's heart is still linked to another.
WATER AIR WATER	Your haste is useless. Your marriage will not last long.
WATER AIR AIR	Yes and soon. The stars are not very friendly with you.
AIR FIRE FIRE	You will see the almond-tree grow many times—but do not despair.
AIR FIRE WATER	Yes, you will marry soon. But why, since you love another?
AIR FIRE AIR	It could be sooner. But you do not seem too good at it.
AIR WATER FIRE	Is not going to be soon. Many

	obstacles will have to be won.
AIR WATER WATER	Wait, wait. In the meantime, ask yourself if you know what you are doing.
AIR WATER AIR	Yes, soon. And a child will follow quickly.
AIR AIR FIRE	Not very soon. Financial and moral difficulties will create doubts in the parents.
AIR AIR WATER	Unfortunately very soon. And you will bitterly repent your decision.
AIR AIR AIR	Many moons will pass before your honeymoon.

RESPONSES TO QUESTION #6

Is my marriage going to be happy?

FIRE FIRE FIRE	Yes, with the exceptions of a few wandering clouds.
FIRE FIRE WATER	Very happy—under one condition. The cradle should not remain empty.
FIRE FIRE AIR	Mutual understanding and tenderness is the path to infinite happiness.
FIRE WATER FIRE	Yes, but you will have to get rid of your useless jealousy.
FIRE WATER WATER	You do not hear the steps in the snow—the same will be for your disputes.
FIRE WATER AIR	Move away from your mutual friendships and your happiness will be complete.
FIRE AIR FIRE	Dawn and sunset will influence

	dramatically your happiness.
FIRE AIR WATER	Moderately. Both of you have to make an effort to make it last.
FIRE AIR AIR	Control your traits. They are very dangerous to a happy ending.
WATER FIRE FIRE	In the first part, the result will deceive you. After words you will have new situations that will improve it.
WATER FIRE WATER	Yes, at the beginning. Then unpleasant discrepancies will make your life miserable.
WATER FIRE AIR	Yes, on the condition that you learn to obey quietly.
WATER WATER FIRE	The icy Siberian wind will not enter your home, if your hands will always hold together.
WATER WATER WATER	No, and the responsibility is your incompatible characters.
WATER WATER AIR	The result will be happy—at the beginning—but for a short time. Make timely arrangements.
WATER AIR FIRE	The result will be positive if you both rely on intelligence and understanding.
WATER AIR WATER	Why are you asking? You know very well, that is not going to be happy.
WATER AIR AIR	How much water do you collect, if you plunge your hands in the river? The same will be for your marriage.
AIR FIRE FIRE	The warm beautiful Crimea's sun will shed happiness on your home.
AIR FIRE WATER	Unavoidable storms will menace your home. Resist and they will disappear.

AIR FIRE AIR	The result is going to be positive, but your restless nature will not appreciate it.
AIR WATER FIRE	Yes, on the condition that relatives and parents stay away from your home.
AIR WATER WATER	Cut your link with your past; the result will depend on this.
AIR WATER AIR	The happy result is conditioned by how both of you control your personalities.
AIR AIR FIRE	A mutual indefinite misunderstanding will undermine form the beginning your happiness.
AIR AIR WATER	The happiness of the result depends on you and you only. Soften your nature and you will see the change.
AIR AIR AIR	Absolutely not. Shortly you will realize why.

RESPONSES TO QUESTION #7

Are my financial struggles going to be over?

FIRE FIRE FIRE	Definitely yes. The favorable turnaround is imminent.
FIRE FIRE WATER	Your perseverance will be faced by alternatives requiring wise judgment and strong nerves.
FIRE FIRE AIR	Do not count on others. Wake up from your lethargy and handle the situation personally.
FIRE WATER FIRE	Evaluate wisely the "time" factor. The next events will work to your favor.

FIRE WATER WATER	Only in part. You will have to fight painfully and for a long period of time.
FIRE WATER AIR	Yes and soon. A providential help will assist you.
FIRE AIR FIRE	Be more patient and more tenacious. The end of your pains is close.
FIRE AIR WATER	Many moons are still to come. Resist with determination and the improvement you are waiting for will finally arrive.
FIRE AIR AIR	You are making a mistake. Change routing and you will see the end of your troubles.
WATER FIRE FIRE	You have too much pride. Continuing in this manner, the result will be zero.
WATER FIRE WATER	The stars are benign. Wait in confidence for a positive change.
WATER FIRE AIR	The chestnuts will have to bloom twice. Wait patiently.
WATER WATER FIRE	Yes and rather soon. A trip will serve to meet your aim.
WATER WATER WATER	Unfortunately not. It is written that your struggles will follow you like your shadow.
WATER WATER AIR	Take the risky way aggressively. The stars are on your side, and will help you.
WATER AIR FIRE	The astrological occurrence is partially hostile. Do not despair, you will end up a winner.
WATER AIR WATER	Your character is weak. In such a situation the fight is long and difficult.
WATER AIR AIR	The situation will improve,

	although not completely. Try to content yourself with such a result.
AIR FIRE FIRE	Continue to fight with faith and don't change your path. Changing now will bring no good.
AIR FIRE WATER	Be patient and resist for some time. New and favorable events are coming.
AIR FIRE AIR	They will certainly be over, but be careful and watch out for possible surprises.
AIR WATER FIRE	The present financial struggles will be over. Unfortunately new ones have to be expected.
AIR WATER WATER	You are hoping in "that" solution. The chance will offer you a new, more attracting one.
AIR WATER AIR	They will be over soon. But you will not find peace of mind.
AIR AIR FIRE	Yours efforts will be successful—keep fighting.
AIR AIR WATER	A friend will help you and your struggles will be over.
AIR AIR AIR	Can you stop the icy northern winds? So it will be for you.

RESPONSES TO QUESTION #8

Will the voyage I am taking meet with favorable results?

FIRE FIRE FIRE	Yes, under all aspects. The stars are on your side.
FIRE FIRE WATER	The results will be positive and you will be compensated for the travel's difficulties.

FIRE FIRE AIR	Start you travel in the same day corresponding to your birth date.
FIRE WATER FIRE	The results will be positive. Control your talking during informal meetings.
FIRE WATER WATER	Ponder over your plans with a cold mind. Is it really worth all this effort?
FIRE WATER AIR	The beginning will be to your advantage—unexpected obstacles will jeopardize the final result.
FIRE AIR FIRE	Your impulsive nature will not help, and the result will be not as good as you may have expected.
FIRE AIR WATER	The oracle's advice is to postpone it —for important personal reasons.
FIRE AIR AIR	The result will not be in line with your expectations and, unfortunately, you are the only one to be blamed.
WATER FIRE FIRE	Go in confidence. Your voyage will help you remarkably.
WATER FIRE WATER	Change your expected departure day with another one. It will be better.
WATER FIRE AIR	Reconsider in detail the planning of your voyage. You need to make some readjustment.
WATER WATER FIRE	Do not postpone it. This is the right time for you.
WATER WATER WATER	Try everything to postpone it. Now it will only damage you.
WATER WATER AIR	The voyage will bring excellent results, but annoying and manipulative companions.
WATER AIR FIRE	Plan your voyage in all details and you will enjoy a very positive

	outcome.
WATER AIR WATER	Postpone the trip to another date. Your health is not at its best.
WATER AIR AIR	You will enjoy the voyage more than its results.
AIR FIRE FIRE	The result is positive, but you will spend a lot of effort to achieve it.
AIR FIRE WATER	The first part will be very tough and full of obstacles. You will have to fight hard and then you will achieve a positive outcome.
AIR FIRE AIR	Be wise and prudent with regards to what you are planning; the voyage is in troubled waters.
AIR WATER FIRE	An unexpected event will modify negatively the desired outcome.
AIR WATER WATER	Your voyage will be useless and you will not meet the expected goals.
AIR WATER AIR	The modest results will not justify the effort you are undertaking.
AIR AIR FIRE	The outcome will be only partially positive and will not coincide with what you have originally expected.
AIR AIR WATER	Make sure your departure date is not corresponding to your birthday.
AIR AIR AIR	Unfortunately the result will be negative. You will see the events run in the opposite direction to what you expected.

RESPONSES TO QUESTION #9

Are my moral struggles going to be over?

| **FIRE FIRE FIRE** | Your nature is too sensitive. |

	Struggles are part of your life.
FIRE FIRE WATER	They are going to be over shortly, provided you really want it.
FIRE FIRE AIR	This is your cross. You are not different from any other human being and you have to carry it.
FIRE WATER FIRE	The big ones will disappear. You will remain with the lesser.
FIRE WATER WATER	Be patient and tenacious. The better days are just around the corner.
FIRE WATER AIR	You have the means to change. Use them and you will see the result.
FIRE AIR FIRE	They will be over when your worst enemy, your character, will be defeated.
FIRE AIR WATER	Listen to the inner voice of your conscience and follow its guidelines; the improvement is there.
FIRE AIR AIR	You can improve the situation with a better soul disposition.
WATER FIRE FIRE	Your moral struggles are imaginary, and your excitable nature has created them.
WATER FIRE WATER	Try the old fashioned smile ... everything will look better.
WATER FIRE AIR	Why so much trouble. Calm yourself, look around and ponder it over.
WATER WATER FIRE	Change your behavior; this will help to end your troubles.
WATER WATER WATER	They will continue, but with time you will learn how to better bear them.
WATER WATER AIR	Just a few moons and your struggles will be over. Take courage.

WATER AIR FIRE	It is written that your struggles are going to end. Keep your morale up.
WATER AIR WATER	Do not be discouraged. Face your hostile destiny with strength and trust , and you will win your fight.
WATER AIR AIR	Your struggles will end one day. Now take your time and do not waste energy. The road is still very long.
AIR FIRE FIRE	Move away from that pessimism. A real friendship will help you to share your pain.
AIR FIRE WATER	The stars are hostile. Analyze candidly your conscience and you may find the answer.
AIR FIRE AIR	Look up and smile at the sun; listen to Mother Nature ... she knows.
AIR WATER FIRE	They will be over, but new ones are coming; so is life.
AIR WATER WATER	Your temperament is weak and irresolute. Find the strength hidden in you and you will succeed.
AIR WATER AIR	Do not let your pride be your only friend. Confide in somebody you trust and you will be understood.
AIR AIR FIRE	Better to drag than to stop; the goal is still ahead.
AIR AIR WATER	Is the "Great River" ever going to be over? So are your struggles.
AIR AIR AIR	They will suddenly be over, like you have been touched by magic.

RESPONSES TO QUESTION #10

Can my physical illness be cured?

FIRE FIRE FIRE	You will be perfectly restored with the help of Divine Providence.
FIRE FIRE WATER	Nature will be your best doctor, and your will be restored.
FIRE FIRE AIR	Yes. Pay attention to the nervous system and the hepatic functions.
FIRE WATER FIRE	Your troubles will be over; be patient and faithful.
FIRE WATER WATER	The initial diagnosis was right. Try natural vegetal treatment in addition.
FIRE WATER AIR	You will get better, but you need time and proper medications.
FIRE AIR FIRE	Your illness is for a great part imaginary.
FIRE AIR WATER	You are in the right direction. Continue the prescribed treatment.
FIRE AIR AIR	You are becoming too discouraged and pessimistic. Retrieve your psychological strength and you will improve.
WATER FIRE FIRE	Your body is not ill. You are suffering from mental fatigue and stress; act accordingly.
WATER FIRE WATER	Control your lifestyle and you will restore shortly.
WATER FIRE AIR	Your problems are not physical. You are a victim of your own extraordinary sensitivity.
WATER WATER FIRE	At the blooming of the chestnuts also your body will bloom.
WATER WATER WATER	You will be restored shortly and remarkably, but not completely.

WATER WATER AIR	You will be restored shortly, but be careful and beware of relapses.
WATER AIR FIRE	Your illness requires a second opinion.
WATER AIR WATER	Why do you complain? These are the logical consequences of your lifestyle.
WATER AIR AIR	Your situation is difficult, but do not despair. The final day is still far away.
AIR FIRE FIRE	Get rid of your melancholy and take courage; your illness will disappear.
AIR FIRE WATER	You have seen too many doctors; the first one was right.
AIR FIRE AIR	You can improve, but you should consider changing your treatment.
AIR WATER FIRE	You do not trust your doctor nor his treatment. How can you be restored?
AIR WATER WATER	Your physical illness has a psychosomatic explanation; see the right doctor.
AIR WATER AIR	The stars are on your side. You will be restored soon and well.
AIR AIR FIRE	Trust your family doctor and the powerful strength of nature.
AIR AIR WATER	You will certainly be restored. Be patient and do not continue to intoxicate your body.
AIR AIR AIR	It is really a difficult task to heal satisfactorily your body.

RESPONSES TO QUESTION #11

Does my dream foretell good?

FIRE FIRE FIRE	Your dream has nothing to do with reality.
FIRE FIRE WATER	The meaning for you is an innervating alternative of worries and serenity.
FIRE FIRE AIR	Your dream is not bringing anything different from the usual flow of events.
FIRE WATER FIRE	It means pains of a short duration, followed by good news and happiness.
FIRE WATER WATER	Unfortunately it means that sad events will hit you shortly.
FIRE WATER AIR	Analyze the synthesis of the dream; the good auspices are very clear.
FIRE AIR FIRE	Be happy. The meaning is a physical and moral improvement in your life.
FIRE AIR WATER	This dream is not at all related to you and your life.
FIRE AIR AIR	The dream means clouds of sadness for you. Fortunately they will be of a brief duration.
WATER FIRE FIRE	Do not be misguided by that dream; the truth will be exactly the opposite.
WATER FIRE WATER	The dream clearly indicated the path you will be following.
WATER FIRE AIR	Your dream is the result of inner worries. Do not take it too seriously.
WATER WATER FIRE	The dream will bring a pleasant financial improvement to your life.
WATER WATER WATER	Your dream is related to events

	concerning one of your relatives.
WATER WATER AIR	The dream means you will have to start a long voyage.
WATER AIR FIRE	Consider carefully the content of your dream and mention it to a loved one.
WATER AIR WATER	It means deception and concern of sentimental nature.
WATER AIR AIR	The stork will fly on to the roof of a house very well known to you.
AIR FIRE FIRE	Call your doctor now. This is what the dream is trying to tell you.
AIR FIRE WATER	The dream is sad. Unfortunately reality will be worse.
AIR FIRE AIR	It means pleasant events of sentimental nature. So, do not worry.
AIR WATER FIRE	A painful situation in your family will follow.
AIR WATER WATER	The dream is bringing sad events to one of your family members.
AIR WATER AIR	Sweet is the dream, bitter the reality.
AIR AIR FIRE	The dream is related to a member of your family.
AIR AIR WATER	Do not take any notice of the content of that dream. Nothing like this is going to happen.
AIR AIR AIR	The dream will bring good news and happy auspices for you and your family.

RESPONSES TO QUESTION #12

Will my premonitions become reality?

FIRE FIRE FIRE	No, so do not worry. You are being influenced by a completely erroneous thought.
FIRE FIRE WATER	Yes it will happen in detail concerning other people directly.
FIRE FIRE AIR	Now you are going too far. Put some order in your thinking, and evaluate the various issues in a positive manner
FIRE WATER FIRE	It is absolutely not possible. You are losing a sense of reality.
FIRE WATER WATER	Yes and soon you will see its natural developments. Still ... be prudent.
FIRE WATER AIR	Your premonition is chaotic and cannot be positively realized.
FIRE AIR WATER	It will very soon become a tough reality. Be prepared for a long and strenuous fight.
FIRE AIR AIR	Unfortunately yes; you need a supportive and generous helping hand.
WATER FIRE FIRE	Your premonition is only the consequence of fears without any logical basis.
WATER FIRE WATER	Yes, it will became reality, but in future times.
WATER FIRE AIR	Yes, it will became reality, and with an impressive similarity in the details.
WATER WATER FIRE	No and be happy. Try instead to improve your shaken nerves.
WATER WATER WATER	It will happen only in part. In any case do not worry too much.

WATER WATER AIR	Why are you so afraid of its logical consequences? You should have been more careful before.
WATER AIR FIRE	It will seem to be true, in a first instance, but then it will change completely.
WATER AIR WATER	The premonition does not concern you directly. Besides, don't you think you are tormenting yourself uselessly?
WATER AIR AIR	It is going to become reality exactly where you are more directly concerned.
AIR FIRE FIRE	Your too fertile fantasy is a real danger to your personality.
AIR FIRE WATER	Stop this thinking. Your premonition is only the consequence of your sensitive nature.
AIR FIRE AIR	Analyze its content and follow the indications. They will bring positive feedback to your life.
AIR WATER FIRE	What you are thinking is not a premonition. You are not well, and this is only a consequence of your physical condition.
AIR WATER WATER	It will become a reality only in those details of lesser importance to you.
AIR WATER AIR	Absolutely not. Consequently do not worry any more.
AIR AIR FIRE	Yes, only partially. Be content, as the stars are in your favor.
AIR AIR WATER	Your premonition is outside the boundaries of what is humanly possible.
AIR AIR AIR	It is going to become reality nearly

in its fullness. So, get ready to handle the logical and practical consequences.

RESPONSES TO QUESTION #13

Will the ill person I am thinking of get well soon?

FIRE FIRE FIRE	Certainly and relatively soon. Be faithful and serene.
FIRE FIRE WATER	A dangerous relapse is to be expected. Take all necessary actions.
FIRE FIRE AIR	The physical strength is still there, but the spirit is hurting the body.
FIRE WATER FIRE	They will get back to normal very, very slowly, and unfortunately not completely.
FIRE WATER WATER	A different climate is needed; act accordingly.
FIRE WATER AIR	Suggest discretely to the person to get another opinion.
FIRE AIR FIRE	It is only a nervous breakdown, and the person will restore well.
FIRE AIR WATER	The person is well treated and in good hands. Divine Providence will do the rest.
FIRE AIR AIR	Dangerous storms are coming. But the person is very strong and will make it.
WATER FIRE FIRE	The danger is in the surgeon's tool; avoid surgery if possible.
WATER FIRE WATER	The worse danger is over; the person will be restored.
WATER FIRE AIR	Suggest a medical joint

consultation; this will be a wise step.

WATER WATER FIRE — The person will be restored and without complicated treatments. So it is written.

WATER WATER WATER — Unfortunately not. Destiny is written in stone.

WATER WATER AIR — Inner moral pains are the real reason for this destroying illness.

WATER AIR FIRE — The celestial writing suggests that the diagnosis should be reviewed.

WATER AIR WATER — Do not despair. Continue diligently with the prescribed treatment.

WATER AIR AIR — The life of the person is in God's hands. Fortunately God is very benign.

AIR FIRE FIRE — Will be restored with the help of a new treatment, more pertinent and powerful.

AIR FIRE WATER — Smile and create smiles. This is the secret for healing that person.

AIR FIRE AIR — The illness is sharp and cutting like a knife. Its name is melancholy.

AIR WATER FIRE — Only an experienced and very talented surgeon can save this person.

AIR WATER WATER — A slow rotation of moons will finally make the desired miracle.

AIR WATER AIR — The possibility to be restored is proportional to the desire to be restored.

AIR AIR FIRE — The person will be restored suddenly and unexpectedly, as by magic.

AIR AIR WATER — The person is, unfortunately, not in good health, and will never fully restore.

AIR AIR AIR	The person will again smile to life. Time and expensive cures are needed.

RESPONSES TO QUESTION #14

What will be the result of my legal issue?

FIRE FIRE FIRE	The result will be positive and you will get full satisfaction.
FIRE FIRE WATER	Try to find a remedy as soon as you can; the adopted strategy is not the most appropriate.
FIRE FIRE AIR	Do not rely completely on your attorney. Be vigilant.
FIRE WATER FIRE	Your adversary is shooting with an unloaded gun. Do not worry.
FIRE WATER WATER	Try to reach an amiable arrangement. All you can get may be considered as a well-found gift.
FIRE WATER AIR	Your adverse party is very tough and astute. Do not under evaluate it and do not over expect.
FIRE AIR FIRE	The result will be quite positive, but you will not receive full compensation.
FIRE AIR WATER	You should hire another layer to assist the one you have now. The issue is too complex for only one attorney.
FIRE AIR AIR	Do not consider yourself the winner. New surprises are on the horizon.
WATER FIRE FIRE	The best solution is to avoid a legal affair. Examine the situation once

	again and decide accordingly.
WATER FIRE WATER	The adverse party has some cunning secret moves. Be prepared to face them.
WATER FIRE AIR	Your adversary is astute and full of resources. I suggest you be prudent and wise.
WATER WATER FIRE	Find an agreement with the opposite party. It is the best solution.
WATER WATER WATER	The fight will be very hard, and your victory only partial.
WATER WATER AIR	Find the best way to reach an arrangement, without lawyers.
WATER AIR FIRE	Find a new strategy and the final victory will be yours.
WATER AIR WATER	Resist but do not risk too heavily; your luck is limited.
WATER AIR AIR	Your adversary starts to feel the fatigue, more than you do. Get together now and try to find an advantageous compromise.
AIR FIRE FIRE	Your attack and defense plans do not seem to be the best. Analyze them once more and find the most suitable solution.
AIR FIRE WATER	The adverse party is cynical and pitiless. Use the same style.
AIR FIRE AIR	Be prompt and give one hand to your adversary. This move will help you a great deal.
AIR WATER FIRE	Your question was bad from the start. It is not wise to insist and take further risks.
AIR WATER WATER	Do not make it too long. Time may work against you.
AIR WATER AIR	Open well your eyes, without

	illusions. Invisible hands are controlling powerful occult interests.
AIR AIR FIRE	The adverse party is protected by the stars and by the words of men.
AIR AIR WATER	Try to obtain diplomatically an arrangement of amiable nature.
AIR AIR AIR	Be prepared for the consequences. The result will be totally negative.

RESPONSES TO QUESTION #15

What will be the result of my project?

FIRE FIRE FIRE	The result of your project will be satisfactory and right on time.
FIRE FIRE WATER	Improve the details and the overall planning, and look with hope and faith to its development.
FIRE FIRE AIR	You cannot build on quicksand. Do not insist and act accordingly.
FIRE WATER FIRE	Your project is weak in its content, but you will be assisted by favorable stars.
FIRE WATER WATER	You are counting too much on imaginary help that you will never receive. Obtain more reliable information and change it suitably.
FIRE WATER AIR	Your project needs basic and immediate modifications. Act fast.
FIRE AIR FIRE	Divine Providence is being benign toward you, even after several mistakes.
FIRE AIR WATER	You can obtain good results, but you need a generous helping hand.

FIRE AIR AIR	Your project is due to fail; to try it is simply foolish.
WATER FIRE FIRE	You will have to wait nervously for several moons, but not in vain. Trust in it.
WATER FIRE WATER	Your project will fail miserably and your pride will be badly shaken.
WATER FIRE AIR	Do not loose your courage and try a different project.
WATER WATER FIRE	Ask for the right support and you will see a successful result.
WATER WATER WATER	Your project requires too much time for its development.
WATER WATER AIR	You have placed a small paper boat in the troubled waters of the Great River.
WATER AIR FIRE	The content of your project is positive; insist with patience and determination, and you will be pleased.
WATER AIR WATER	If you expect a rich harvest, you need to carry out a good and timely job of sowing.
WATER AIR AIR	The result of your project will be modest. Be content with it, as it is the best you can reach.
AIR FIRE FIRE	Only a miracle can make it work and the miracle will happen.
AIR FIRE WATER	Many, many obstacles will deliberately be placed in your way.
AIR FIRE AIR	Do not have too many illusions about its result, but get ready with a new and more pragmatic project.
AIR WATER FIRE	Rivalry and envy will make the result difficult and stressful.
AIR WATER WATER	Your fiery and obstinate nature will face a terrible task; continue with

	unchanged faith.
AIR WATER AIR	You talk too much to the wrong people. Be careful, otherwise you can be betrayed and badly hurt.
AIR AIR FIRE	A long and great fight is awaiting you, but the final result is worth the effort.
AIR AIR WATER	You will see many successions of snow and grain, but one day it will be your day.
AIR AIR AIR	The result of your project will be very disappointing for you.

RESPONSES TO QUESTION #16

Are my misfortunes going to end?

FIRE FIRE FIRE	You can consider yourself a very lucky person: the answer is "very soon."
FIRE FIRE WATER	Yes, but look over your shoulder; others are coming.
FIRE FIRE AIR	The winter season finally ends, and spring arrives. Unfortunately winter will come back.
FIRE WATER FIRE	Time will turn your hair gray, but will bring serenity to your soul.
FIRE WATER WATER	Very often your misfortunes are just a consequence of your character.
FIRE WATER AIR	They will stop momentarily, but then new ones will hit you.
FIRE AIR FIRE	Sooner than you think. The oncoming events will be very favorable.
FIRE AIR WATER	Not completely, but your life will

	definitely get better. Be faithful.
FIRE AIR AIR	Remove the wrinkles from your forehead and smile. The end is not too far away.
WATER FIRE FIRE	Look behind the limits of this material situation, and you will see the desired end.
WATER FIRE WATER	Your cross will be with you for some more time. Be patient and persist.
WATER FIRE AIR	The more serious will be soon over, only the minor will continue to worry you.
WATER WATER FIRE	Take courage and continue your journey. The end is not too far away.
WTER WATER WATERA	Your stars are benign and favorable. Wait for a little more.
WATER WATER AIR	A calm sea is followed by the storm; so is your life and so it will continue to be.
WATER AIR FIRE	Silent tears will be in your eyes for sometime. So it is written.
WATER AIR WATER	Be more aggressive and find new strength. Misfortunes like weak people.
WATER AIR AIR	Stop telling them to others. What advantage or help are you getting?
AIR FIRE FIRE	Maintain your pace and be more faithful. Life has some good news for you.
AIR FIRE WATER	Your life will be followed by misfortunes like by a shadow.
AIR FIRE AIR	Bigger misfortunes are hitting people more important than you. Maybe this consideration can help you a little.
AIR WATER FIRE	Your misfortunes can reproduce

	themselves, according to your mood.
AIR WATER WATER	Find you lost faith and your misfortunes will end.
AIR WATER AIR	You are responsible for most of your misfortunes. It is useless to complain now.
AIR AIR FIRE	Lean strongly on somebody and you will be able to move out from this negative path.
AIR AIR WATER	Have you ever asked yourself: do I deserve to be exempt by misfortunes?
AIR AIR AIR	Your stars are looking in other directions and your pain will continue to stay with you.

RESPONSES TO QUESTION #17

Will the person I am living with always be faithful?

FIRE FIRE FIRE	Will be always faithful and pays you back with gratitude.
FIRE FIRE WATER	Be content with what you have, it is more than you deserve.
FIRE FIRE AIR	Your unreasonable jealousy might, one day, push the person to betray you.
FIRE WATER FIRE	Watch out for your friendships and you will receive steady faithfulness.
FIRE WATER WATER	Increase the warmth of your love. You will be paid back accordingly.
FIRE WATER AIR	Control and improve your behavior, if you want your wish to become true.

FIRE AIR FIRE	Feed the love incessantly and do not trouble your trust with doubt.
FIRE AIR WATER	Always? Your stars are giving me controversial answers.
FIRE AIR AIR	Improve your character. This will eliminate an existing danger.
WATER FIRE FIRE	Take their hands into yours and kiss them. This gesture is well deserved.
WATER FIRE WATER	Always? Yes. Try to honor this gift with your conscience.
WATER FIRE AIR	Your selfish and suspicious nature is tormenting you uselessly.
WATER WATER FIRE	Brighten the road of faithfulness with your most sincere and constant smile.
WATER WATER WATER	Is going to be faithful, even if you do not deserve it.
WATER WATER AIR	Beware of the gossip coming from unfriendly people who only want to spread dangerous poison.
WATER AIR FIRE	Keep this question to you. The person you think is above all suspects.
WATER AIR WATER	Jesus Christ said once "only he who never sinned may throw the first stone."
WATER AIR AIR	Look at this person deep in the eyes, you will understand ...
AIR FIRE FIRE	Faithfulness has an expensive price: you are very stingy. Take then the right action.
AIR FIRE WATER	Maybe they are not going to be always faithful, but they will always love you.
AIR FIRE AIR	Your abnormal sensitivity is going to damage you and your lover's life.
AIR WATER FIRE	The absolute faithfulness is a myth;

	exactly the same as yours.
AIR WATER WATER	The human nature of the person is weak, but the soul is stronger.
AIR WATER AIR	Show clearly and openly your love, there will be no time left to think otherwise.
AIR AIR FIRE	Why such a fear? Be close to the person and show your love at all times.
AIR AIR WATER	Your concerns have no grounds. This person is much better than you.
AIR AIR AIR	And why should this person be always faithful? What will be the advantage?

RESPONSES TO QUESTION #18

Is my life going to be financially prosperous?

FIRE FIRE FIRE	Your stars are strong and will protect you. Do not worry.
FIRE FIRE WATER	Do not throw time and efforts away. Your destiny is in mediocrity.
FIRE FIRE AIR	Your selfish nature will be a hindrance to a joyful and serene life.
FIRE WATER FIRE	You will have to wait for many moons before reaching prosperity.
FIRE WATER WATER	The road will be long and painful; but finally you will find prosperity.
FIRE WATER AIR	Your life is bound to prosperity; but you will have to fight hard to get it.
FIRE AIR FIRE	You will reach the desired objective when, unfortunately, it will be too

	late.
FIRE AIR WATER	Alternatives of good and bad luck will be a characteristic of your destiny.
FIRE AIR AIR	Do not despair if you do not see the light, suddenly it will shine.
WATER FIRE FIRE	You are the only captain of your ship. Act accordingly in a wise and fast manner.
WATER FIRE WATER	Your unusually sensitive nature will damage a prosperity which seemed almost there.
WATER FIRE AIR	You will reach prosperity in an unexpected and unbelievable way.
WATER WATER FIRE	Stop for a minute and relax. One day you will reach your goal.
WATER WATER WATER	Yes, but only if you will show determination in facing several difficulties.
WATER WATER AIR	It is difficult to look forward to a prosperous life, if you have lost confidence in yourself.
WATER AIR FIRE	You will reach prosperity only thanks to your personal abilities.
WATER AIR WATER	Look at yourself. Are you really trying so hard to deserve it?
WATER AIR AIR	Your life is bound to prosperity. The problem will be to maintain it.
AIR FIRE FIRE	What you see far away is not a mirage. Continue to fight and you will reach it.
AIR FIRE WATER	You will reach prosperity, thanks to generous friends.
AIR FIRE AIR	Keep steady the wheel of your ship. You will win the storm and reach calm sea.
AIR WATER FIRE	Your spouse will bring you the

	prosperity you are looking for.
AIR WATER WATER	The events of your life will go through a series of lucky opportunities.
AIR WATER AIR	Your will is weak and you are a big spender. How can you ever think about prosperity.
AIR AIR FIRE	Keep your health, your lively spirit and a few doubloons. This is all you need.
AIR AIR WATER	In my land they say "Sow wisely and the harvest will be golden."
AIR AIR AIR	Watch out for the unforeseen. One day your good stars will abandon you.

RESPONSES TO QUESTION #19

Am I going to have children and will they bring joy to me?

FIRE FIRE FIRE	You will have both children and joy. The stars are with you.
FIRE FIRE WATER	Go with the small number. The responsibility of raising them is going to be very hard for you.
FIRE FIRE AIR	The satisfaction you will receive from your children will be the prize for your remarkable efforts in raising them.
FIRE WATER FIRE	Not many, but of excellent breed. You should thank your lucky stars.
FIRE WATER WATER	More girls than boys.
FIRE WATER AIR	As it happens in life, some of them will be good, some not.
FIRE AIR FIRE	Yes, and when grown-up they will

	give you enough joy to compensate so many sleepless nights.
FIRE AIR WATER	They will be excellent, but you will not be able to raise them in an excellent way.
FIRE AIR AIR	Yes but... their characters will give you lots of headaches.
WATER FIRE FIRE	More boys than girls.
WATER FIRE WATER	Yes and one in particular will gratify you.
WATER FIRE AIR	Your children will be sort of rebels, but you will be a good parent.
WATER WATER FIRE	Two, but as troublesome as ten.
WATER WATER WATER	It is written: a few children—a lot of satisfaction.
WATER WATER AIR	Only one, who will keep you company during your old days.
WATER AIR FIRE	Not more than one, but no regrets, it will be enough.
WATER AIR WATER	Three and for two of them you will cry a lot, for joy and for sorrow.
WATER AIR AIR	Yes, and one of them will make your life sad and miserable.
AIR FIRE FIRE	Just a few, and they will make your life happy, with the exception of one.
AIR FIRE WATER	I see none in your future, but probably this will be better for you.
AIR FIRE AIR	Two. When small they will give you pain, when grown-up they will give you joy.
AIR WATER FIRE	Very difficult it will be for you to have children. This will be your secret pain.
AIR WATER WATER	You will have your well deserved satisfactions, but only after many troubles.

AIR WATER AIR	Yes and when they are small they will cheer your life. Then specific events will bring changes.
AIR AIR FIRE	Three. And for two of them your soul will tremble many times.
AIR AIR WATER	Only one, and with a destiny that will lead away from you.
AIR AIR AIR	So it is written: many children, but just a few joys from them.

RESPONSES TO QUESTION #20

Do I have loyal and generous friends?

FIRE FIRE FIRE	You can consider yourself a very lucky person. Your friends are loyal and generous.
FIRE FIRE WATER	Loyal and generous? I do not think so. Pay more attention to your friends.
FIRE FIRE AIR	They are very loyal. Unfortunately it is impossible for them to be generous.
FIRE WATER FIRE	Why are you asking this question? Look to your inner self and not in the mirror.
FIRE WATER WATER	You only have superficial acquaintances, not real friends.
FIRE WATER AIR	Beware of friends of the feminine sex, better the other one.
FIRE AIR FIRE	Yes, they are. They also would like you to reciprocate in kind.
FIRE AIR WATER	You cannot distinguish between good and bad friends. Your intuition is failing.

FIRE AIR AIR	Only one is loyal and generous. The others are just the opposite.
WATER FIRE FIRE	Yes. You, on the contrary, are at fault, because of your suspicious and selfish nature.
WATER FIRE WATER	Once you had some. Now you have lost them. Try to think about this.
WATER FIRE AIR	You often get transported by a sort of sentimental romanticism. This is a danger in a friendship.
WATER WATER FIRE	When with you they blame others. The other way round when they are with others.
WATER WATER WATER	Be more attentive in the choice of your friends. Some of them are really excellent.
WATER WATER AIR	Among those that you think you know the answer is negative. Look harder elsewhere.
WATER AIR FIRE	Your friendships have a morbid background and you do not seem to realize it. Beware.
WATER AIR WATER	Yes, certainly. But do not take advantage with selfish motives.
WATER AIR AIR	Your friends are superficial. You find it out when you will need them most.
AIR FIRE FIRE	Yes. Unfortunately unforeseen events will take away the best.
AIR FIRE WATER	Your friends will negatively expose you. Be wiser and more careful.
AIR FIRE AIR	If you are inclined to love, then keep your friends.
AIR WATER FIRE	Beware of those of masculine sex. For you female friends are better.
AIR WATER WATER	Loyal and generous? What did they do for you when you needed them?

AIR WATER AIR	Yes, they are. But one day they will be fed up with you, because of your behavior.
AIR AIR FIRE	Yes and also very patient to bear your faults.
AIR AIR WATER	Your friends are only good with words. Get some better ones.
AIR AIR AIR	Beware of your so-called friends. They are moody and disinterested.

RESPONSES TO QUESTION #21

Am I lucky at gambling?

FIRE FIRE FIRE	Very lucky in a very unforeseen manner.
FIRE FIRE WATER	Luck is fickle—do not count too much on it.
FIRE FIRE AIR	Be ready and persistent. One day you will make it.
FIRE WATER FIRE	Your audacity does not meet your goals. Better a wise prudence.
FIRE WATER WATER	Your financial improvement will be caused by a manifestation of luck.
FIRE WATER AIR	Try and do not despair. One day Lady Luck will come to you.
FIRE AIR FIRE	Even if sometimes you win, be careful, and do some math.
FIRE AIR WATER	Do not risk too hard. This can be a source of damage for you.
FIRE AIR AIR	You win only when you cheat. One-day people will find out.
WATER FIRE FIRE	Stop gambling. Your luck will reach you by a different road.
WATER FIRE WATER	You lack in the pleasure of risk and

in persistence. Be more optimistic and you will see the result.

WATER FIRE AIR Yes, the big day of your luck will come. You have only to be patient and wait ...

WATER WATER FIRE Gambling for you is like a slow poison. One day it will finally kill you.

WATER WATER WATER In gambling you will only see a small portion of luck.

WATER WATER AIR Do not overdo it and try to keep the right balance. You must only gamble for fun.

WATER AIR FIRE When your desperation reaches a climax, then you will see victory.

WATER AIR WATER You are wasting your best hours and your best efforts in gambling.

WATER AIR AIR The green carpet fascinates you like the eyes of the cobra.

AIR FIRE FIRE Beware of the "roulette" ball. One day it will drive you crazy.

AIR FIRE WATER Your happy moment is expected to arrive: so it is written. You just have to wait and to trust.

AIR FIRE AIR If you really want to give it a try, do it with the cards, not at the green tables.

AIR WATER FIRE Somebody will advise you on how to make a small fortune.

AIR WATER WATER Gamble, but know when you have to stop.

AIR WATER AIR If you are looking for the destruction of your home and your family, then continue to gamble.

AIR AIR FIRE You are too sensitive and emotional. Try other pastimes.

AIR AIR WATER Gamble, but go easy with betting. I

AIR AIR AIR   know it is difficult, but it is my best advice. Would you be successful if you fought a giant? So it is with gambling.

RESPONSES TO QUESTION #22

Will I travel extensively in the near future?

FIRE FIRE FIRE	You will travel beyond the Eastern and Western boundaries.
FIRE FIRE WATER	Business travels will take you to faraway countries.
FIRE FIRE AIR	Family and business will be the reason for your many travels.
FIRE WATER FIRE	Your imaginative spirit would like to travel, but your lazy body does not.
FIRE WATER WATER	Very limited will be your traveling, and you will regret it. I suggest you not to, because this is much better for you.
FIRE WATER AIR	Unforeseen events will impose on you long and stressing travels.
FIRE AIR FIRE	Many voyages, most of them into your mind.
FIRE AIR WATER	Family reasons will oblige you to many travels; often uselessly.
FIRE AIR AIR	Your lover will make you travel a lot.
WATER FIRE FIRE	The death of important people will be a reason for your many travels.
WATER FIRE WATER	Business trips will alternate with pleasure trips.

WATER FIRE AIR   Political events will oblige you to leave your country.

WATER WATER FIRE   You have a nomadic nature. Your life is a continuous journey.

WATER WATER WATER You will travel a lot in your own country.

WATER WATER AIR   Your life's events will oblige you to several travels. Beware, as one trip will be very dangerous.

WATER AIR FIRE   Financial reasons will make you travel for long voyages around the world.

WATER AIR WATER   Not many and you will regret it.

WATER AIR AIR   The most traveling is already behind you.

AIR FIRE FIRE   Good and enjoyable friends will cause you to travel a lot.

AIR FIRE WATER   Two forced trips will cause you sorrow and pain.

AIR FIRE AIR   One trip could be the last one. Beware!

AIR WATER FIRE   Many travels, but one only that you will remember forever.

AIR WATER WATER   You will want to stop, but this will be impossible.

AIR WATER AIR   Be wise and prudent in your traveling. One voyage can be very dangerous.

AIR AIR FIRE   A forced trip you were opposed to, will, on the contrary, bring you happiness and prosperity.

AIR AIR WATER   Not many, but all pleasant and rich with different experiences.

AIR AIR AIR   Your future will not bring you particularly meaningful trips.

RESPONSES TO QUESTION #23

Does the person I love correspond to me?

FIRE FIRE FIRE	You are reciprocated with love and tenderness.
FIRE FIRE WATER	You are sincerely loved, but not really trusted.
FIRE FIRE AIR	The person you love is tormented by inner and dangerous doubts.
FIRE WATER FIRE	Your love is being reciprocated now, but somebody is trying to change the mind of the person you love.
FIRE WATER WATER	The person you love is studying you and analyzing your behavior.
FIRE WATER AIR	The person loves you, but is too reserved to show it.
FIRE AIR FIRE	The shadow of another person is in between you two; but you are being equally loved.
FIRE AIR WATER	You are reciprocated sentimentally, but not sexually.
FIRE AIR AIR	Mutual friends are an obstacle to an increased reciprocity.
WATER FIRE FIRE	You are being loved sincerely now, but the situation will be modified in the future.
WATER FIRE WATER	The person loves you. You are not realizing it properly because of their attitude.
WATER FIRE AIR	Do not expect more than what is shown. This person is not capable of loving more.
WATER WATER FIRE	Pretend a certain coolness. This old move will work once again.
WATER WATER WATER	The person you love, loves you with a sort of prudent reserve.

WATER WATER AIR	The person really loves you. It is your character that makes this relation so difficult.
WATER AIR FIRE	A lot physically, not very much sentimentally.
WATER AIR WATER	Do not insist. This person's heart belongs to a luckier one.
WATER AIR AIR	Strict parents are working against you.
AIR FIRE FIRE	The person does not reciprocates your love as yet. In the future you will see a change.
AIR FIRE WATER	The person is reciprocating your love for a practical reason. There is still nothing for you to worry about and you should calm yourself.
AIR FIRE AIR	Show your love more clearly. This will provoke a better and clearer reciprocity.
AIR WATER FIRE	You are loved with such a magnitude, that I wonder if you deserve it.
AIR WATER WATER	Some interested parties are trying to change the feeling of the person you love. Act fast and accordingly.
AIR WATER AIR	The person has loved too much in the past. This is making things more difficult.
AIR AIR FIRE	Do not lose your self confidence and continue with your tenderness. One day you will see the good results.
AIR AIR WATER	The person is looking after you with sincere affection. But this is not really true love.
AIR AIR AIR	Beware of the person you are in

love with. You are not being at all reciprocated.

RESPONSES TO QUESTION #24

Will I inherit real estate properties?

FIRE FIRE FIRE	Yes, and of an outstanding value. Unfortunately it will happen too late and they will be useless.
FIRE FIRE WATER	It will be just a very little thing. So let's wake up and do not dream in vain.
FIRE FIRE AIR	Try to keep them wisely and devotedly. They have been created with great efforts.
FIRE WATER FIRE	Yes you will. These properties will be like a condemnation to you.
FIRE WATER WATER	Yes. Please remember those who left them to you, at least once a year.
FIRE WATER AIR	What are you expecting them for? You know that you are not capable of running them.
FIRE AIR FIRE	Financial interests will destroy the good spirit of familiar sentiments.
FIRE AIR WATER	Yes and it will cost you a large part of your flesh.
FIRE AIR AIR	Certainly not. But your life will be prosperous thanks to your efforts.
WATER FIRE FIRE	Yes and they will bring you various and long lasting problems.
WATER FIRE WATER	The person sharing your life will leave them to you one day and you will live in prosperity.
WATER FIRE AIR	Many, many. Enough to make your

	doctor and your attorney two very rich persons.
WATER WATER FIRE	Very little and not so interesting. Watch out for your old age.
WATER WATER WATER	You should. But expect to see them disappear in legal questions.
WATER WATER AIR	You will. And your inheritance on earth will came along with bitter pains.
WATER AIR FIRE	Absolutely not. Count only on your personal gains.
WATER AIR WATER	Yes, under the condition that you find the strength to fight for them.
WATER AIR AIR	Yes and from that moment on, the poor people will knock in vain at your door.
AIR FIRE FIRE	Nothing in financial good, a lot in spiritual wealth.
AIR FIRE WATER	Yes but only in exchange for a person that you love so deeply.
AIR FIRE AIR	An implacable storm will bring into dust what you have inherited.
AIR WATER FIRE	Yes, one day. Do not dissipate your inheritance on bad financial speculations.
AIR WATER WATER	Give a part of them to charity. This was the untold desire of the person who left them.
AIR WATER AIR	From a fistful of gold to a handful of dust, the road is very short.
AIR AIR FIRE	Clean them with generous charities. They smell the dirt.
AIR AIR WATER	No, but do not worry. You will not need them.
AIR AIR AIR	Plenty, and unfortunately you will not have the time to enjoy them. Your heirs will.

RESPONSES TO QUESTION #25

Do I have many enemies and are they dangerous?

FIRE FIRE FIRE	Many, some known and some unknown. All extremely dangerous.
FIRE FIRE WATER	Keep your mind awake and ready to fight. You will be able to destroy them easily.
FIRE FIRE AIR	Relax and do not worry. The worst of them have already disappeared.
FIRE WATER FIRE	Their number is not an issue. They can be scared away by a flock of sheep.
FIRE WATER WATER	The worse ones are those very close to you. Keep your eyes very open.
FIRE WATER AIR	Just a few women, but their revenge is great and pitiless.
FIRE AIR FIRE	Your enemies are trying to scare you with an unloaded gun. You can make fun of them.
FIRE AIR WATER	The worst are among your close relatives. Watch out!
FIRE AIR AIR	They used to be just a few. Now they have multiplied.
WATER FIRE FIRE	Your enemies can dangerously hit you. But you too have some arrows in your bow.
WATER FIRE WATER	Prevent them from grouping together. It is easier to defeat them one by one.
WATER FIRE AIR	A few men. Very vindictive and not used to forgiving.
WATER WATER FIRE	If the rabbit is scaring you, then you

should be scared of your enemy.

WATER WATER WATER Much more than you can think of, and also extremely dangerous.

WATER WATER AIR Renew your old friendships and your fears will go away.

WATER AIR FIRE Not many; but those few are as violent as buffaloes.

WATER AIR WATER Just a few. Be patient and they will disappear one after the other.

WATER AIR AIR Reinforce your friendships. This will annihilate your enemies.

AIR FIRE FIRE You are a neutral person. No friends, no enemies.

AIR FIRE WATER Many but all very scared of you. They will never find the courage to strike you.

AIR FIRE AIR Only one, very powerful. Your own character.

AIR WATER FIRE Only two: a man and a woman. Beware of them. They are waiting for the most suitable moment to hit you.

AIR WATER WATER The winter and the wind of the steppe are equal to your enemies in their toughness.

AIR WATER AIR Plenty and making a lot of noise like hens in the coop. This is not a great danger.

AIR AIR FIRE Give your hand wisely and generously. This will disarm your enemy.

AIR AIR WATER Beware of your false friends rather than your enemies.

AIR AIR AIR Much less than what you may expect, and really inoffensive.

RESPONSES TO QUESTION #26

Will I be able to retire one day under good financial conditions?

FIRE FIRE FIRE	Do not make useless dreams; you will be required to work and fight all your life.
FIRE FIRE WATER	If you want to ensure a prosperous retirement, do not attempt to try complex financial speculations.
FIRE FIRE AIR	Do not count on other people's help and one day you will succeed.
FIRE WATER FIRE	Why are you looking for financial prosperity? You will not be able to enjoy it ...
FIRE WATER WATER	One day your arid selfishness will bring this gift to you.
FIRE WATER AIR	Beware of one of these elements: air —fire—water. One of them will damage your wealth.
FIRE AIR FIRE	You will be able to make it, if you continue to take advantage of the misery of your servants.
FIRE AIR WATER	Enlarge the scenario of your business. This will help you to reach your goal.
FIRE AIR AIR	You will not have the time. It will stop you before you reach your goal.
WATER FIRE FIRE	You do not have too much luck and your future welfare is uncertain.
WATER FIRE WATER	Your safe will be full when your hair is gray.
WATER FIRE AIR	Change your character and your lifestyle and you will succeed.
WATER WATER FIRE	One day you will make it, but you

will have to go through many tough fights.

WATER WATER WATER   Yes under the condition that you can save money wisely.

WATER WATER AIR   If you do not make it, it will not be your fault. The stars are not on your side.

WATER AIR FIRE   Yes, but the only condition is that you decide to better control your own interests.

WATER AIR WATER   Beware. Unforeseen problems and family difficulties will hinder your projects.

WATER AIR AIR   Yes and unfortunately only your doctors will take advantage of it.

AIR FIRE FIRE   Yes, but find the right time to retire.

AIR FIRE WATER   Listen to the advice of the person you are sharing your life with. You will make it.

AIR FIRE AIR   You certainly have many good qualities and one day you will be touched by luck.

AIR WATER FIRE   Control more attentively the persons working for you. This will save you.

AIR WATER WATER   Yes. Avoid legal questions and beware of lawyers.

AIR WATER AIR   Listen to my words: you will get what you have given.

AIR AIR FIRE   Fight against your secret vice. This is the real enemy to your projects.

AIR AIR WATER   Concentrate the focus of your attention only on your financial interests. This will make you wealthy.

AIR AIR AIR   You can certainly count on it. Therefore you can even be generous with yourself.

RESPONSES TO QUESTION #27

Is my reputation enjoying esteem and trust?

FIRE FIRE FIRE	Your friends and your enemies evaluate you in the same manner.
FIRE FIRE WATER	Slow down with your pride and your ambition. You will see your reputation improving.
FIRE FIRE AIR	It will, if you have the courage to get rid of all those false friends and flatterers.
FIRE WATER FIRE	Not really. The problem is what is exuding from your double life.
FIRE WATER WATER	It will, if you are able to intelligently come out from your present situation.
FIRE WATER AIR	A little with your friends, much more with your enemies.
FIRE AIR FIRE	A lot, particularly among those who do not know you so well.
FIRE AIR WATER	Your reputation is in decline. Act accordingly.
FIRE AIR AIR	Yes, provided you give to the poor what you take away from the rich.
WATER FIRE FIRE	Low esteem and trust with the people of your sex. Better with those from the opposite sex.
WATER FIRE WATER	How can you expect it, if you do not get back on the right track.
WATER FIRE AIR	Yes, thanks to your consummate ability to lie.
WATER WATER FIRE	Some with the persons of your sex.

	Less with the others.
WATER WATER WATER	No illusions. Little esteem and even less trust.
WATER WATER AIR	Look out and defend yourself. Your reputation is the object of a great hate and envy.
WATER AIR FIRE	Yes, according to your right value.
WATER AIR WATER	Yes, but please abandon those friends with dirty hands.
WATER AIR AIR	Yes, only when your hair will become gray.
AIR FIRE FIRE	Keep the good reputation of your family and be content with it.
AIR FIRE WATER	More among foreigners than among your own people.
AIR FIRE AIR	Yes and it will improve as long as your deeds will.
AIR WATER FIRE	Your reputation was much better in the past. Now is declining.
AIR WATER WATER	Very little among those that know you well.
AIR WATER AIR	Build a granitic pedestal with good, sincere and generous gestures.
AIR AIR FIRE	Yes, for a little while. Think about rapidly changing your residence and your habits.
AIR AIR WATER	Not very much at present. You have the qualities to improve it in the future.
AIR AIR AIR	The icy wind of the steppe has a better reputation than you.

RESPONSES TO QUESTION #28

What will the near future bring me?

FIRE FIRE FIRE	Events charged with premonitions of deception.
FIRE FIRE WATER	Moral satisfactions for you and your family.
FIRE FIRE AIR	Sentimental relations very important to your future.
FIRE WATER FIRE	Troubles and pain caused by your irregular behavior.
FIRE WATER WATER	Forced residence changes that will be favorable to your future.
FIRE WATER AIR	Important voyages regarding the development of your business.
FIRE AIR FIRE	Unpleasant communications that will increase your nervous stress.
FIRE AIR WATER	Positive meetings opening to new opportunities.
FIRE AIR AIR	A lot of sacrifice and of stress and then a certain well being for you.
WATER FIRE FIRE	Remarkable disappointments for you and members of your family.
WATER FIRE WATER	Sentimental relations characterized by limited success.
WATER FIRE AIR	New and positive acquaintances in the sentimental field.
WATER WATER FIRE	Small events in different fields, to bring you joy.
WATER WATER WATER	Very decisive events for your future.
WATER WATER AIR	An amazing revamping of old interests, completely forgotten by you.
WATER AIR FIRE	Unpleasant surprises that will modify for worse the present situation.

WATER AIR WATER	Dangerous voyages unfavorable to your safety.
WATER AIR AIR	Legal questions and affairs that will resolve positively for you.
AIR FIRE FIRE	Sentimental encounters which bring sadness.
AIR FIRE WATER	A pleasant surprise will make your life better.
AIR FIRE AIR	Alternative events will bring good and bad.
AIR WATER FIRE	Fights and stress, fortunately only for a short time.
AIR WATER WATER	Change of residence not favorable and even dangerous for your future.
AIR WATER AIR	Alternatives of success and failure, in different fields, will shock you.
AIR AIR FIRE	Legal questions caused by your superficial nature.
AIR AIR WATER	Useless voyages dangerous to your social status.
AIR AIR AIR	Nothing. Nothing really worth mentioning.

RESPONSES TO QUESTION #29

Is the person who is faraway thinking about me, and will they come back?

FIRE FIRE FIRE	The person is not thinking about you and will not come back.
FIRE FIRE WATER	The person remembers you with indifference and will come back for convenience.
FIRE FIRE AIR	They are remembering you with hate, and coming back to punish

	you.
FIRE WATER FIRE	Remembrances are weak and the return will be just to leave you again.
FIRE WATER WATER	The person is not remembering you nor coming back? What have you done to deserve this?
FIRE WATER AIR	The person is constantly thinking of you, but cannot come back.
FIRE AIR FIRE	The reminder is great as well as the coming back.
FIRE AIR WATER	The person is not thinking about you, but is coming back.
FIRE AIR AIR	Another person is in between and hinders remembrance and return.
WATER FIRE FIRE	One day they will remember you. One day they will come back repentant.
WATER FIRE WATER	The person remembers you, but you have lost it. Pity.
WATER FIRE AIR	The person remembers you all the time, and will suddenly return.
WATER WATER FIRE	You have hurt the person too deeply, so do not expect a quick return.
WATER WATER WATER	The memories are confused and coming back is very doubtful.
WATER WATER AIR	Major interests are hindering thought and returns.
WATER AIR FIRE	You are remembered with feeling, but do not expect a return.
WATER AIR WATER	Send appropriate messages to let this person know that you remember. Their return will come with joy.
WATER AIR AIR	You are remembered yes, but a major force is hindering their

	return.
AIR FIRE FIRE	Price is hindering their return. One-day love will do the work.
AIR FIRE WATER	Your behavior is not helping a good memory, nor a return.
AIR FIRE AIR	The memory is superficial, and the return will last only a short time.
AIR WATER FIRE	The memory is full of resentment, the return is extremely difficult.
AIR WATER WATER	You are remembered with love, and you will see the person very soon.
AIR WATER AIR	The character of the person is, as you know, strange and unusual. Both memory and return seem impossible.
AIR AIR FIRE	New events have cancelled the memory and hinder the return.
AIR AIR WATER	Sexual attraction will be the reason for the return.
AIR AIR AIR	The person cannot remember you. You will see them again in spirit.

RESPONSES TO QUESTION #30

How will my name and my works be judged by the posterity?

FIRE FIRE FIRE	Your works will be judged at the same level as your name.
FIRE FIRE WATER	Posterity will be generous and respectful of your works.
FIRE FIRE AIR	Posterity's judgment? Poor the name, the same for the works.
FIRE WATER FIRE	It will all depend on what you will be able to do in the next year.
FIRE WATER WATER	The first part of your life will be

	ignored. The second will receive respect and honor.
FIRE WATER AIR	Your works are bound to stay. Your name will be forgotten.
FIRE AIR FIRE	The winds of the steppe created in hate will be storming against your name and your works.
FIRE AIR WATER	You will be criticized, praised and destroyed like all mortals.
FIRE AIR AIR	Cancel your past with positive deeds. You will be remembered well.
WATER FIRE FIRE	Your implacable enemies will oblige posterity to neglect your name.
WATER FIRE WATER	The best part of you will resist the test of time.
WATER FIRE AIR	Posterity will be a severe judge. You do not deserve otherwise.
WATER WATER FIRE	You will be remembered for a short time. Do not worry and try to create something meaningful for yourself.
WATER WATER WATER	Posterity will only judge your works and completely neglect your name.
WATER WATER AIR	Posterity will be critical of your name and your personal character, but will respect your works.
WATER AIR FIRE	If by "posterity" you mean "your family" then you will be remembered in a very positive way.
WATER AIR WATER	If you insist on the road that you have undertaken, what type of judgment do you expect?
WATER AIR AIR	Posterity will not understand your works, and will soon forget your name.
AIR FIRE FIRE	Your name and your works will be

	destroyed by the terrible strength of calumny.
AIR FIRE WATER	Not the name, nor the works will remain. They have been written on the desert's sand.
AIR FIRE AIR	Those who did not really know you too well, will keep a good memory of you.
AIR WATER FIRE	Your name and your works will be engraved in granite.
AIR WATER WATER	All of you, name and works, will be forgotten very soon like a meteor in the sky.
AIR WATER AIR	Posterity will only remember your negative points, and will forget the positive ones.
AIR AIR FIRE	Many people will try to cancel your impressive work.
AIR AIR WATER	Your family will endeavor tenaciously to obtain respect for you and your work.
AIR AIR AIR	No judgment. Complete neglect will reign on all you did.

RESPONSES TO QUESTION #31

Will I witness political or military changes?

FIRE FIRE FIRE	Not only witness, you will also play a role in the new events.
FIRE FIRE WATER	You will witness certain changes, but do not worry, your stars will protect you.
FIRE FIRE AIR	Political changes is unavoidable. Do not get involved and it will be better

	for you.
FIRE WATER FIRE	Yes, and you will be violently taken in, against your will.
FIRE WATER WATER	There will be change. But fortunately for you, you will be hidden in a sure place.
FIRE WATER AIR	You will witness great political changes.
FIRE AIR FIRE	Yes. And your wise nature will give you the best advice on how to handle the new situation.
FIRE AIR WATER	Important events will modify the assets of your family.
FIRE AIR AIR	The changes you will witness, will bring positive improvements.
WATER FIRE FIRE	Yes. And your astute and cunning nature will guide you in time.
WATER FIRE WATER	You will witness political changes, but fortunately for you, not military.
WATER FIRE AIR	The changes will be so great, that you will be very alarmed.
WATER WATER FIRE	Yes and without having to wait too long. Be prepared for the consequences.
WATER WATER WATER	To witness is to say the least. You will have to bear painful consequences.
WATER WATER AIR	Yes. Face them with wise spirit and they will not touch you.
WATER AIR FIRE	Because of events, your familiar life will undergo painful situations.
WATER AIR WATER	No, but your nerves will not bear the long waiting and the terrible uncertainty.
WATER AIR AIR	The political changes will be quite normal and will be under the control of your superiors.

AIR FIRE FIRE	Yes and because of mistakes made by the ruling class of your country.
AIR FIRE WATER	The political changes you will witness will bode ill for you.
AIR FIRE AIR	Your luck will protect you, but not your children.
AIR WATER FIRE	Political changes will oblige you to move to a foreign country.
AIR WATER WATER	Yes and plentiful, but not so dangerous and basically useless.
AIR WATER AIR	One only, but very important for you and for your fellow countrymen.
AIR AIR FIRE	The political changes you are waiting for will never succeed.
AIR AIR WATER	Two political events will avoid a military action.
AIR AIR AIR	A cruel and pitiless enemy will enter your house as the boss.

RESPONSES TO QUESTION #32

Will I marry the "ideal?"

FIRE FIRE FIRE	If by "ideal" you mean a lot of money, then the answer is yes.
FIRE FIRE WATER	If you can control your expectations, you will be successful.
FIRE FIRE AIR	Wait patiently for the time assigned by your favorable destiny.
FIRE WATER FIRE	It will seem the "ideal" to you, but you will then regret the choice.
FIRE WATER WATER	Your weak and difficult nature will distort the possibility to handle the situation.

FIRE WATER AIR	Yes you will. But your character will change the person.
FIRE AIR FIRE	If you can renounce to "youth" you can certainly marry the "ideal."
FIRE AIR WATER	How can you hope to deserve this gift reserved to happy few?
FIRE AIR AIR	Many moons will cross the sky, and finally luck will be on your side.
WATER FIRE FIRE	The present opportunity is probably the best you can reach. Consider it seriously.
WATER FIRE WATER	Your excessive sensitivity will be an obstacle to this difficult choice.
WATER FIRE AIR	Impossible. You will have to build it with your hands.
WATER WATER FIRE	If you will only superficially love the person you are going to marry, then this can be your "ideal."
WATER WATER WATER	What do you mean by "ideal?" A person to understand you? In this case the answer is yes.
WATER WATER AIR	No illusions. In the sky something else is written.
WATER AIR FIRE	Your ideal is only a dream. And usually one wakes up abruptly from dreams.
WATER AIR WATER	Yes, if you will remove that band of pride from your eyes.
WATER AIR AIR	Choose freely and quietly, you will be lucky.
AIR FIRE FIRE	It may be not your "ideal," but it will be a great love.
AIR FIRE WATER	You will be following it for all your life, without reaching it. Pity.
AIR FIRE AIR	In destiny it is written that you will transform the person you will marry.

AIR WATER FIRE	Yes. But after a while the person will become very common.
AIR WATER WATER	Only a partial "ideal." This is the best you can expect.
AIR WATER AIR	Do not look too high. The "ideal" has your size.
AIR AIR FIRE	Ask your heart in depth and the choice will be easier.
AIR AIR WATER	A person with your character cannot expect too much. You do not deserve a miracle.
AIR AIR AIR	What do you mean by "ideal?" A person that can bear you? If this is the case, the answer is positive.

RESPONSES TO QUESTION #33

Am I going to be lucky in love?

FIRE FIRE FIRE	You will have a great luck, even if you certainly do not deserve it.
FIRE FIRE WATER	Your luck will be mediocre, but continuous and without highs and lows.
FIRE FIRE AIR	Your luck will be similar to a discordant sway.
FIRE WATER FIRE	Your special luck in love will be called "wealth."
FIRE WATER WATER	Very little and you will have to fight a lot to maintain it.
FIRE WATER AIR	Yes and plentiful in the first part of your life.
FIRE AIR FIRE	The name of your luck in love is "faithfulness."
FIRE AIR WATER	Many years will pass. Wait and you

	will be happy one day.
FIRE AIR AIR	Yes, but you have to improve your own character.
WATER FIRE FIRE	Moderately. Still you will be required to fight, because of many rivalries.
WATER FIRE WATER	Lucky in the small sentimental stories, but unlucky in the great love story.
WATER FIRE AIR	Luck will come close to you many times. Keep your eyes open and do not let it run away.
WATER WATER FIRE	Your second love will be the lucky one, and will cure the pains of the first.
WATER WATER WATER	No. The stars do not seem on your side.
WATER WATER AIR	The name of your luck in love is "adultery."
WATER AIR FIRE	Do a small gesture of understanding and luck will become your friend.
WATER AIR WATER	You will have the luck you desire. Unfortunately you will not be able to keep it.
WATER AIR AIR	Your luck in love will be the consequence of an unforeseen voyage.
AIR FIRE FIRE	The person sharing life with you, will be your true "luck."
AIR FIRE WATER	Look attentively around you. Luck is very close.
AIR FIRE AIR	Unforeseen events will transform the unlucky situation into a lucky one.
AIR WATER FIRE	Yes and people will envy you a lot because of this.

AIR WATER WATER	The volubility of your nature will be an obstacle to your luck.
AIR WATER AIR	Many opportunities for a lucky choice, but you will not be capable of choosing.
AIR AIR FIRE	Your luck in love is far away. Away from your own country.
AIR AIR WATER	"Chance" will constantly influence the lucky events of your love affairs.
AIR AIR AIR	You will be lucky in love only when it is too late.

RESPONSES TO QUESTION #34

Will I move to a foreign country?

FIRE FIRE FIRE	Yes, and in this foreign country you will find prosperity and the end of your mortal life.
FIRE FIRE WATER	Certainly, but your voyage will be long, fatiguing and useless.
FIRE FIRE AIR	You will be very tempted to do it. Think well before deciding.
FIRE WATER FIRE	Yes. And on the new country you will find delusions and regrets.
FIRE WATER WATER	Come back soon. The foreign people will not be friendly or helpful.
FIRE WATER AIR	It will not be a permanent change of residence, only a temporary stay.
FIRE AIR FIRE	Do not stay too long. This wise decision will maintain your wellbeing.
FIRE AIR WATER	Absolutely not. You are not in a position to do it.

FIRE AIR AIR	Stay where you belong. Your own country will compensate you.
WATER FIRE FIRE	Yes, but the secret "nostalgia" of your own country will break your heart.
WATER FIRE WATER	Do not let temptation try you. On the contrary it will be a great mistake.
WATER FIRE AIR	Certainly one day, but against your will.
WATER WATER FIRE	Do not cross the boundaries of your own country. This will not be good for you.
WATER WATER WATER	Yes, and in the foreign country you will find love and happiness.
WATER WATER AIR	Yes but remember that the return will not be possible.
WATER AIR FIRE	Your change of residence will be caused by family reasons.
WATER AIR WATER	You will, and you will also come back very sadly.
WATER AIR AIR	Your transfer will last just a few years.
AIR FIRE FIRE	Yes, notwithstanding the opposition of your parents and relatives.
AIR FIRE WATER	Very sad events will be the only reason for you to move.
AIR FIRE AIR	Yes and this will greatly improve your personal business.
AIR WATER FIRE	You will move, but under the influence of illogical thinking.
AIR WATER WATER	Yes, and the person you love will despair.
AIR WATER AIR	Yes, but you will have to wait, for a long time, before you can make it.
AIR AIR FIRE	No. Unforeseen events will change plans at the last moment.

AIR AIR WATER	Yes and nobody will regret your departure. So it is written.
AIR AIR AIR	It will not be a voluntary move, but an exile.

RESPONSES TO QUESTION #35

Are my descendants going to be happy after my death, and will they remember me?

FIRE FIRE FIRE	Your destiny will change, and only then they will realize your value.
FIRE FIRE WATER	They will fight over the inheritance and they will negatively judge your actions.
FIRE FIRE AIR	They will dissipate the inheritance and will neglect your remarkable efforts.
FIRE WATER FIRE	They will multiply their investments, following closely your advice.
FIRE WATER WATER	They will destroy all that you have created and will forget all your teachings.
FIRE WATER AIR	Their life will be easy and superficial, and they will only slightly remember you.
FIRE AIR FIRE	Your house will be abandoned and nobody will bring flowers to your tomb.
FIRE AIR WATER	They will work hard and with good results. They will have great respect for your name.
FIRE AIR AIR	They will live honestly and discreetly. Your name will

	be remembered for a long time.
WATER FIRE FIRE	Each of them will follow his own path. They will continue not to understand you, as before.
WATER FIRE WATER	They will fight very hard, and finally they will understand your sacrifices.
WATER FIRE AIR	They will live badly and will believe that you did not do enough for them.
WATER WATER FIRE	Their lifestyle will change, and they will start to understand the pain of missing you.
WATER WATER WATER	Their existence will be happy, and they will honor your memory.
WATER WATER AIR	They will live serene and happy, and will honor you on the day of their deaths.
WATER AIR FIRE	They will be lucky and happy. Only one will remember you.
WATER AIR WATER	Their life will be very turbulent and they will have no time to remember you.
WATER AIR AIR	They will not be lucky. They will blame you, not rightly so, for this.
AIR FIRE FIRE	They will remember that you are not there anymore, only because their prosperity will diminish.
AIR FIRE WATER	They will live selfishly and will judge very severely your innate generosity.
AIR FIRE AIR	Their existence will be very alternate, and so their memory of you.
AIR WATER FIRE	Their life will be superficial and the memory of you very short.
AIR WATER WATER	They will not be successful and this

	is partially your fault. But they will never blame you for this.
AIR WATER AIR	They will dissipate your wealth, and make ironical comments on your avarice.
AIR AIR FIRE	Successful but sad. Constantly remembering what you did for them.
AIR AIR WATER	Prosperous and very involved in charities, mainly to change your reputation.
AIR AIR AIR	They will not be very prosperous, and they will blame you for their sad destiny.

RESPONSES TO QUESTION #36

Is my life going to be bustling?

FIRE FIRE FIRE	Bustling is to say the least. You can add "restless and innervating."
FIRE FIRE WATER	The stars are on your side and will protect you. Go ahead on your path and do not be scared.
FIRE FIRE AIR	The person sharing your life with you will make sure that is going to be bustling.
FIRE WATER FIRE	Look at the movement of the snow in the storm and wind. So will be your life.
FIRE WATER WATER	The union with a wise person will give the needed brake to your restless life.
FIRE WATER AIR	The first part will be similar to lead, the second to mercury.

FIRE AIR FIRE	Your life will quiet and serene, but not for your merit.
FIRE AIR WATER	Your youth will bustle disorderly, your maturity will be calm, and you will precociously get old.
FIRE AIR AIR	It will be restless and bustling because of your character.
WATER FIRE FIRE	Learn how to pick up your friends. Your existence will be happy and serene.
WATER FIRE WATER	Try to find an honest and methodical job. On the contrary you will regret it.
WATER FIRE AIR	Will run crazily like a fox followed by hounds.
WATER WATER FIRE	Cure your nervous system, or you will risk a lot.
WATER WATER WATER	There will be very bustling periods, followed by very quiet ones, but with an apparent and anxious calm.
WATER WATER AIR	It will depend a great deal on your will. I suggest you better control yourself.
WATER AIR FIRE	Have you seen the bears jumping on the burning charcoal. So will be your life.
WATER AIR WATER	You are following a path that will take you to the earthquake.
WATER AIR AIR	It certainly will be a little bustling. And you will greatly enjoy that "little."
AIR FIRE FIRE	It will be disastrously bustling and you will not escape this written destiny.
AIR FIRE WATER	Look in the sky at the clouds vainly followed by the wind. So is your life.

AIR FIRE AIR	You are excessively sensitive. Your life will be in accordance.
AIR WATER FIRE	Your life will be similar to the water in the pond. Do not worry.
AIR WATER WATER	Pleasant and unpleasant events will make it very bustling and interesting.
AIR WATER AIR	Yes, very bustling. And you will never get bored.
AIR AIR FIRE	Your existence will go through unforeseen changes and shake-ups.
AIR AIR WATER	One day you will face a crossroad. Choose the less adventurous road.
AIR AIR AIR	Think about the great oppressing silences of my land. So will be your life.

RESPONSES TO QUESTION #37

Are calumnies against my person going to damage my career and life?

FIRE FIRE FIRE	Only one, but very heavy and dangerous for your life.
FIRE FIRE WATER	No. Your personality will successfully oppose their negative impact.
FIRE FIRE AIR	They will not damage you. Their action will be limited to a restricted circle.
FIRE WATER FIRE	No. You will change your residence in the right and suitable time.
FIRE WATER WATER	A few snow flakes do not stay too long under the sun's rays.
FIRE WATER AIR	Yes, only in part. Your future deeds

	will bring your reputation back.
FIRE AIR FIRE	Yes. These accusations will obtain the goals desired by your enemies.
FIRE AIR WATER	Undoubtedly, given also the nature of your character you tend to get umbrageous for no reason.
FIRE AIR AIR	No, with regard to the effects on your family. Yes, to the effect on your acquaintances.
WATER FIRE FIRE	Have you seen a stone in the pond. The effect will be very similar.
WATER FIRE WATER	They will unavoidably bring a certain concern, but of a limited dangerous effect.
WATER FIRE AIR	They will damage your person in a remarkable way, because of your special nature.
WATER WATER FIRE	Yes, like a stone thrown with force against a surface made of crystal.
WATER WATER WATER	A little, but in a cutting and subtle manner that will wound you like a scalpel.
WATER WATER AIR	Do not be afraid. Your sincere friends will intervene and will rehabilitate your reputation.
WATER AIR FIRE	They will be similar to light plumes and they will not even touch you.
WATER AIR WATER	Try to remain strong and indifferent. Offenses will not damage granite.
WATER AIR AIR	You will tremble from the difficulty, but you will be able to stand up, calm and strong.
AIR FIRE FIRE	You can balance very well in difficult situations, and will be able to find a clever way out.
AIR FIRE WATER	They will not damage you, because

	you will not even know them.
AIR FIRE AIR	Defend yourself and do not go down easily. You will reduce the damage to a minimum.
AIR WATER FIRE	They will be like the punctures of a pin, too soft for your tough skin.
AIR WATER WATER	Termites always bring damages; but there are ways to protect your house and yourself.
AIR WATER AIR	No fear and no regrets. The truth will always come to light on the side of the just person.
AIR AIR FIRE	No. They will destroy themselves against your granitic reputation.
AIR AIR WATER	Yes, in part, because it will be uneasy for you to prove your innocence.
AIR AIR AIR	No false accusations will touch you. Your skin is tough and you resemble the Siberian bear.

RESPONSES TO QUESTION #38

Will I receive an important communication, and what will be the content?

FIRE FIRE FIRE	They will bring news of a great joy for you.
FIRE FIRE WATER	You will receive news whose content will be in the opposite direction to what you were expecting.
FIRE FIRE AIR	You will receive communications of a very annoying content.
FIRE WATER FIRE	Unpleasant news. But do not worry

too much, as better ones will follow them in the near future.

FIRE WATER WATER They will bring information which you will find useful, precious and advantageous for your business.

FIRE WATER AIR You will receive a letter that will oblige you to make a long voyage.

FIRE AIR FIRE Yes, advantageous for your projects, but not good in the sentimental area.

FIRE AIR WATER The communication you will receive is very important for your future.

FIRE AIR AIR Yes. Specific communications will oblige unforeseen expenses.

WATER FIRE FIRE Yes and they will contain boring invitations and propositions. Do not even reply.

WATER FIRE WATER They will ask you for important commitments. Give a negative answer.

WATER FIRE AIR You will receive a letter for which you have been waiting a long time.

WATER WATER FIRE Yes. Not good for your business; but pleasant for your sentimental life.

WATER WATER WATER It will bring sad news for you and your family.

WATER WATER AIR Yes. Communications which will enable you to collect old debts.

WATER AIR FIRE You will receive a communication very positive for your family.

WATER AIR WATER Yes, but do not haste. Think deeply and attentively before answering.

WATER AIR AIR You will receive letters with unpleasant news. People who are dear to you are ill.

AIR FIRE FIRE They will contain information of no

	use to you.
AIR FIRE WATER	The communication you will receive will oblige you to cancel a planned trip.
AIR FIRE AIR	Yes. Anonymous letters. Read them only once and then throw them away.
AIR WATER FIRE	You will receive an unexpected letter containing a pleasant invitation.
AIR WATER WATER	Yes. Offensive communications. A wise and long analysis will help you to see the situation in the right perspective.
AIR WATER AIR	You will receive pleasant news from an old friend nearly forgotten.
AIR AIR FIRE	You will receive a letter with an unpleasant invitation for you.
AIR AIR WATER	You will receive news and communications very advantageous to your social status.
AIR AIR AIR	The news you are going to receive will cause a dangerous situation.

RESPONSES TO QUESTION #39

What will be the consequences of the damage I have suffered?

FIRE FIRE FIRE	Very serious, but with a fast remedy.
FIRE FIRE WATER	Not much for you, but it will cause a lot of talking from your acquaintances.
FIRE FIRE AIR	Because of your sensitive nature, they will cause damage at the psychological level.

FIRE WATER FIRE	Act immediately and the consequences will be under control soon.
FIRE WATER WATER	The consequences will be borne only by the members of your family.
FIRE WATER AIR	You will not notice the damage. Do not worry.
FIRE AIR FIRE	Do not torment yourself. No serious consequences. You will recover soon.
FIRE AIR WATER	The damage will only create a certain nervousness.
FIRE AIR AIR	Remarkable. They will influence heavily your spouse.
WATER FIRE FIRE	None. As usual you tend to exaggerate and over imagine.
WATER FIRE WATER	Thank your stars for what happened. You will learn to be more wise and prudent.
WATER FIRE AIR	The damage will cause serious consequences of a physical nature.
WATER WATER FIRE	Act immediately to repair it. You will avoid a worse situation.
WATER WATER WATER	The natural consequences will bring a certain unbalance in your business.
WATER WATER AIR	What is your fear? The sting from a mosquito certainly does not cause great pain.
WATER AIR FIRE	The damage will only bring transient consequences for the short term.
WATER AIR WATER	The consequences will be light. Smile, nobody will notice.
WATER AIR AIR	For you none. The consequences will be born by your creditors.
AIR FIRE FIRE	The logical consequence will be a

	voyage that you will start soon.
AIR FIRE WATER	The damage will not prejudice your personal reputation.
AIR FIRE AIR	The damage will be felt by your pride. You will have to ask for help from other people.
AIR WATER FIRE	No consequences with a really negative effect. Your position is strong and reliable.
AIR WATER WATER	Do not worry. The damage will turn into an advantageous development for you.
AIR WATER AIR	Sleep and relax in peace. You will rapidly recover your loss somewhere else.
AIR AIR FIRE	Do not torment yourself. You can count on good and generous friends.
AIR AIR WATER	No really serious consequences. The stars are on your side.
AIR AIR AIR	The consequences will be felt more at moral than at financial level.

RESPONSES TO QUESTION #40

Will I have to fight with a rival?

FIRE FIRE FIRE	Yes, and it will be a useless fight, without any chance of success.
FIRE FIRE WATER	Use your good and generous spirit. This tool will help you to win.
FIRE FIRE AIR	Yes and because of your hypersensitive nature, you will lose in a series of wrong moves.
FIRE WATER FIRE	Yes but do not worry. You are an

	athlete very expert in this specialty.
FIRE WATER WATER	This is my advice. At the suitable time, use only your brain.
FIRE WATER AIR	Be prepared as the fight will be with more than one rival.
FIRE AIR FIRE	Listen to me: be wise and avoid the fight. It will be better for you.
FIRE AIR WATER	You will defeat the rival you are fearing now. Another one, even more dangerous, will appear
FIRE AIR AIR	Can you defend yourself from the icy wind of the steppe? So it will be for you.
WATER FIRE FIRE	Your fight will be long and tough, but, unfortunately, useless.
WATER FIRE WATER	The rival is strong. But your innate stubbornness even stronger.
WATER FIRE AIR	You may win only by using tact and diplomacy.
WATER WATER FIRE	Rivals? Nobody can really compete with you. Do not worry.
WATER WATER WATER	Yes and a deceptive victory will be the result of the fight.
WATER WATER AIR	Yes and with great torment. Can you fairly fight with a spirit?
WATER AIR FIRE	Yes and concede soon. There is little you can do to defend yourself.
WATER AIR WATER	Yes and it will be a desperate fight, without exclusion of mortal moves.
WATER AIR AIR	Many moons will pass before you can defeat your rival.
AIR FIRE FIRE	Yes and during the fight you will have to use the astuteness of the fox and the strength of the bear
AIR FIRE WATER	Be prepared for the fight. Only with a great deal of patience and tenacity you will be able to win.

AIR FIRE AIR	Yes and when the fight is over, you will understand that you fought in vain.
AIR WATER FIRE	Yes, but do not be afraid. You have the stronger personality.
AIR WATER WATER	Yes and it will be a stressful fight, with no winners and no losers.
AIR WATER AIR	Yes, but do not worry. Powerful friends will help you tremendously.
AIR AIR FIRE	Yes and unfortunately this is the type of fight where you are not strong enough.
AIR AIR WATER	No. You do not have rivals to be concerned about.
AIR AIR AIR	Yes, but no fear. Your victory will be total and easy.

RESPONSES TO QUESTION #41

Will I be happy after the changes in my present situation?

FIRE FIRE FIRE	Undoubtedly. The change will totally modify your existence.
FIRE FIRE WATER	An inner secret delusion will hinder the appreciation of your change.
FIRE FIRE AIR	Because of your innate selfishness the new situation will end up as a confused compromise.
FIRE WATER FIRE	The change will not satisfy your unrealistic expectations.
FIRE WATER WATER	Nobody will believe it. But you will be feeling really happy.
FIRE WATER AIR	You will not be completely happy, but much happier than before.

FIRE AIR FIRE	If you will be capable of being content, you will find something very close to happiness.
FIRE AIR WATER	The change will not really modify your present lifestyle.
FIRE AIR AIR	Your character will hinder reaching the desired happiness.
WATER FIRE FIRE	You will not really be happy, but everybody will believe you are.
WATER FIRE WATER	You will often think: I was better before.
WATER FIRE AIR	Certainly not immediately. You will be happier only after a few years.
WATER WATER FIRE	You, very little. But the people living with you will be really happy.
WATER WATER WATER	You will always be the unsatisfied and restless person that you are.
WATER WATER AIR	The change will suggest the path to real happiness.
WATER AIR FIRE	Not immediately, as you hoped. You will have to wait for a few moons.
WATER AIR WATER	The change will make you happy. But you will have to fight hard to keep your happiness.
WATER AIR AIR	The change in your present status, will be the happiness of your family.
AIR FIRE FIRE	It is not the change that will make you happy, but your children.
AIR FIRE WATER	The change will bring money, but not the happiness you were expecting.
AIR FIRE AIR	You will be really happy, but not those living with you.
AIR WATER FIRE	A concern will secretly shadow your happiness: your parents.
AIR WATER WATER	You will be an envied person, but not a really happy one.

AIR WATER AIR	It is not the change that will make you happy, but the events happening after.
AIR AIR FIRE	A painful flaw will hinder your happiness: your jealousy.
AIR AIR WATER	Happiness will not be the result of change, but the person you will meet will cause it.
AIR AIR AIR	You will bitterly regret your situation before the change.

RESPONSES TO QUESTION #42

Is the person I am thinking about going to be helpful?

FIRE FIRE FIRE	The person will be very useful, and you can count on it also for the future.
FIRE FIRE WATER	Yes, you can count on it. But consider that what will be done, is not going to be enough for you.
FIRE FIRE AIR	The person will be useful by means of a precious suggestion.
FIRE WATER FIRE	They will be useful, but very expensive.
FIRE WATER WATER	No. One of your enemies will tell the person not to help you.
FIRE WATER AIR	Useful with words, yes. Not with facts.
FIRE AIR FIRE	If you can, do without this person. The help that you may receive will be very expensive for you.
FIRE AIR WATER	Useful. Meaning that you will receive financial help.
FIRE AIR AIR	Not very useful. On the contrary,

	you will lose precious time.
WATER FIRE FIRE	Yes, but through time consuming and innervating diplomacy.
WATER FIRE WATER	The person will honestly try to be helpful, with very little results.
WATER FIRE AIR	Yes, the person will be very helpful, but be prepared to pay a very heavy price.
WATER WATER FIRE	My sincere advice? The true friendship is a myth.
WATER WATER WATER	They will only be partially useful. More than that will not be possible.
WATER WATER AIR	The person will help you. But you will bitterly regret that you ever asked.
WATER AIR FIRE	They will be useful, but your back will have to bow down to the floor.
WATER AIR WATER	Yes. But you cannot count on total confidentiality.
WATER AIR AIR	The person will introduce you to another who can really be of help.
AIR FIRE FIRE	The person might be useful, but under unacceptable conditions.
AIR FIRE WATER	They will be useful, but your personal pride will be seriously shaken by them.
AIR FIRE AIR	I suggest that you direct your attention toward another person.
AIR WATER FIRE	One day the person will be useful; but you will get very tired of waiting.
AIR WATER WATER	You can count on it. The help will arrive only indirectly.
AIR WATER AIR	They will be useful if you do not ask too much. Think well before formulating your needs.
AIR AIR FIRE	The help will arrive when your

	hopes will be nearly vanished.
AIR AIR WATER	Not immediately. The help will only arrive in the midterm. Be patient.
AIR AIR AIR	Do not count too much on it. Otherwise the disappointment will be unbearable.

RESPONSES TO QUESTION #43

Will I keep my present position?

FIRE FIRE FIRE	You will not only keep it, but you can improve it even more.
FIRE FIRE WATER	Do not rest on your laurels. Be prepared to defend your position.
FIRE FIRE AIR	You will keep it, if you leave apart your ambitions for the future.
FIRE WATER FIRE	No, you will return back only when the current of the river will be favorable.
FIRE WATER WATER	Undoubtedly. Your eloquence is really worth a kingdom.
FIRE WATER AIR	Yes, but be careful not to make dangerous moves. Be prudent.
FIRE AIR FIRE	Do not have many illusions. Your basis is made of soft clay.
FIRE AIR WATER	You will keep it, only by using the difficult art to balance in strong winds.
FIRE AIR AIR	Look well at your shoulders, otherwise you will lose it.
WATER FIRE FIRE	Yes, but somebody will have to sacrifice for you.
WATER FIRE WATER	Do not worry. The wind will blow on your favor for many springs.

WATER FIRE AIR	You will make it, thanks to your astute mind.
WATER WATER FIRE	Your boat is very steady and will resist the terrible storm.
WATER WATER WATER	Continue with your harmonious lifestyle, and you will be able to keep it.
WATER WATER AIR	You will keep it for long, notwithstanding envious people.
WATER AIR FIRE	Yes. With a great effort and a lot of energies spent.
WATER AIR WATER	No and you will move a few steps down in the social ladder.
WATER AIR AIR	You will keep it. Control your pride and give your hand to your adversaries.
AIR FIRE FIRE	Yes. A person of the opposite sex will be of a great help.
AIR FIRE WATER	You will keep it thanks to the continuous and generous support from your relatives.
AIR FIRE AIR	It is possible. Observe the wise work of the ants.
AIR WATER FIRE	Yes, but you will have to ask for help from your best friends.
AIR WATER WATER	No, for a few moons, the stars will move away from you.
AIR WATER AIR	Wear your high boots. Your path is crossed by high waters.
AIR AIR FIRE	Only in part. Gray and stormy clouds will cross your sky for a while.
AIR AIR WATER	You will keep it for others. For you the situation will be different.
AIR AIR AIR	It will not be possible. It will suddenly escape like a sweet-water fish.

RESPONSES TO QUESTION #44

Is the person I am thinking about going to be fortunate?

FIRE FIRE FIRE They will be very successful, but only by moving to a foreign country.

FIRE FIRE WATER One day. The time has not yet come. Be patient.

FIRE FIRE AIR Yes, only by associating with other people.

FIRE WATER FIRE Very limited success for this person, who is not the only one to be blamed for it.

FIRE WATER WATER Yes, but only under the condition that this person will get rid of all their bad habits.

FIRE WATER AIR The person will have really deserved success.

FIRE AIR FIRE A lot at the beginning. Things will then change and you will see more ups and downs. Be careful.

FIRE AIR WATER The success will arrive only if the person knows how to be consistent in the daily fight of life.

FIRE AIR AIR The stars of this person have arranged for a succession of triumphs and failures.

WATER FIRE FIRE Certainly a prosperous lifestyle, not a great success.

WATER FIRE WATER The person will not be capable of earning a remarkable wealth.

WATER FIRE AIR If you are able to support this person during their life, then the

	answer is "yes."
WATER WATER FIRE	Suggest that this person not leaves his/her country. One day you will be thanked for this.
WATER WATER WATER	Certainly, but this person will have to listen to your suggestions.
WATER WATER AIR	One day, yes. And that day will be very sad for you.
WATER AIR FIRE	Certainly, but going through difficult and hostile situations.
WATER AIR WATER	The person will find success away from you. Do not worry, because the person will then came back.
WATER AIR AIR	Listen: even the young of the forest bear need some help.
AIR FIRE FIRE	Do not look forward to this day, because you will lose the person.
AIR FIRE WATER	The person will have to patiently wait for his/her turn: so it is written.
AIR FIRE AIR	This person will have a certain fortune, not in gambling nor in risky speculations, but through hard work.
AIR WATER FIRE	Yes. Under the only condition that this person is able to overcome strong initial difficulties.
AIR WATER WATER	Listen: the young child can walk if you hold him with your hand.
AIR WATER AIR	Yes, but without entering in a joint venture with other people. This will be a danger.
AIR AIR FIRE	This person will not have their deserved fortune. Pity.
AIR AIR WATER	Very little. The road started is leading to a dead end.
AIR AIR AIR	No. And it is very dangerous to try to force your own destiny.

RESPONSES TO QUESTION #45

What is my true character?

FIRE FIRE FIRE	The question is useless. You do not have a real character.
FIRE FIRE WATER	Fair. And the transformation is due to the intelligent work of your relatives.
FIRE FIRE AIR	Observe with attention how your friends behave towards you and you will understand better your character.
FIRE WATER FIRE	Really bad. Your parents bear the fault for having spoiled you.
FIRE WATER WATER	Take away a piece of pride, and add some common sense.
FIRE WATER AIR	You will never know. He that knows you well will never tell you.
FIRE AIR FIRE	Cut, with courage, imagination from reality, and your character will be normal.
FIRE AIR WATER	Your character is the slave of your hypersensitive nature.
FIRE AIR AIR	The unbalance between optimism and pessimism is very dangerous for the harmonious development of your character.
WATER FIRE FIRE	A real disaster. And your friends are at fault because they have always tolerated you.
WATER FIRE WATER	Your character is similar to a blind man trying to walk desperately without his cane and his dog.

WATER FIRE AIR	Your character is the unconscious victim of your whimsical nature.
WATER WATER FIRE	Your character is too much under the strong influence of the Moon.
WATER WATER WATER	Do not be too overindulgent and be more self-critical.
WATER WATER AIR	Too many ups and downs will seriously damage your character.
WATER AIR FIRE	Your character is a prisoner of other people's will.
WATER AIR WATER	Your character is dualistic. One for your and one for the others.
WATER AIR AIR	You have a bad opinion of it, but the real truth is even worse.
AIR FIRE FIRE	It is an excellent character. Unfortunately you made yourself to be judged very differently.
AIR FIRE WATER	Your character is prisoner of controversial and paradoxical complexes.
AIR FIRE AIR	Please do not ask me this question. I know that you would not like the truth.
AIR WATER FIRE	A latent destroying jealousy is slowly deforming your real character.
AIR WATER WATER	Your character? You mean what is "left" of it?
AIR WATER AIR	Your character changes constantly with the rotation of the moon.
AIR AIR FIRE	You think is excellent. It is even better.
AIR AIR WATER	It is similar to the actors roles. Changing according to the play.
AIR AIR AIR	Your is not a very clear character, but a confused mosaic.

RESPONSES TO QUESTION #46

What will be the result of the speculative transaction I have planned?

FIRE FIRE FIRE	The result will be the one you desire.
FIRE FIRE WATER	The result will be very modest because if interference of rivals.
FIRE FIRE AIR	The result will be no gain, no loss.
FIRE WATER FIRE	Mediocre. Unforeseen negative events will modify the expected result.
FIRE WATER WATER	Good, although part of the gains will move into other people's hands.
FIRE WATER AIR	The result will be unexpectedly good.
FIRE AIR FIRE	The result will be positive. But will cost you a quantity of troubles and pains.
FIRE AIR WATER	Change your project. This speculation is not going to bring you wealth.
FIRE AIR AIR	The result will be proportional with the risk you have taken.
WATER FIRE FIRE	The final result will make you wait. But finally will be positive.
WATER FIRE WATER	Excellent. Unfortunately you will have to share the interests with another person.
WATER FIRE AIR	Abandon this project. These types of speculations are not made for you.
WATER WATER FIRE	The result will make more noise than money.
WATER WATER WATER	The result will be negative.
WATER WATER AIR	The result will be in great part

good, and will be the prize of your obstinacy.

WATER AIR FIRE — Abandon it. If you insist you will only collect bitter deceptions.

WATER AIR WATER — Work out in better detail your project, and the speculation that will follow, will be successful.

WATER AIR AIR — Once again the stars will be on your side. Do not worry.

AIR FIRE FIRE — No fear. Your nose is typical of an old fox, and will not betray you.

AIR FIRE WATER — The speculation is good. Wait patiently for the right time, which is coming.

AIR FIRE AIR — The result will be good, but you have to content yourself with the minimum.

AIR WATER FIRE — The result will less than your too optimistic forecast.

AIR WATER WATER — You will be pleased with the result, but you have to reduce the range of risk.

AIR WATER AIR — The speculation you have planned will oblige you to try a second one, very soon.

AIR AIR FIRE — You will collect substantial results only with some patience.

AIR AIR WATER — The result will be positive, but you have to make special arrangements.

AIR AIR AIR — Your speculation will have no result. It will remain an aborted project.

RESPONSES TO QUESTION #47

What is the true character of the person I am thinking of?

FIRE FIRE FIRE	It is exactly the opposite of what it seems.
FIRE FIRE WATER	Good in the overall. But you have to understand it correctly.
FIRE FIRE AIR	It is exactly what it is shown.
FIRE WATER FIRE	Indifference and superficiality are the main characteristics.
FIRE WATER WATER	The true character is what your intuitive nature has understood.
FIRE WATER AIR	The character of this person is absolutely not suitable for you.
FIRE AIR FIRE	A suggestion? Be content with what it appears to be.
FIRE AIR WATER	The true character will be unbearable for you.
FIRE AIR AIR	Wait a few moons. The true character will be a surprise for you.
WATER FIRE FIRE	The excesses of the Moon are making the true character of this person.
WATER FIRE WATER	Nothing unusual. A very normal and plain character.
WATER FIRE AIR	The character of this person will easily dominate you.
WATER WATER FIRE	The character is basically good. Unfortunately their emotions are controlled by the bear
WATER WATER WATER	The true character is better that what it is seems.
WATER WATER AIR	The character is similar to virgin wax. You will have to mold it.
WATER AIR FIRE	Analyze the person attentively and you will notice that the character is

	as spicy as "paprika."
WATER AIR WATER	Do not torment yourself. You will take it as it is.
WATER AIR AIR	Good in general. The difficult thing is to find out from what side to approach it.
AIR FIRE FIRE	At the beginning it was a wonderful character. It has been changed by a series of negative events.
AIR FIRE WATER	The true character is hidden by a false masque.
AIR FIRE AIR	The answer is easy: very similar to yours. Think about it.
AIR WATER FIRE	The character would be great. Unfortunately the weakness is damaging it.
AIR WATER WATER	The true character is still not completely formed.
AIR WATER AIR	Your question is useless. You are not interested in the character, but in the person.
AIR AIR FIRE	Not bad. Basically it is the character of a very spoiled person.
AIR AIR WATER	My advice? Do not look for details and you will live a better life.
AIR AIR AIR	The person is missing what is considered a true and determined character.

RESPONSES TO QUESTION #48

Will I be successful in a sport or entertainment career?

FIRE FIRE FIRE	Do not attempt to try any of these careers. You will be wasting your

	time.
FIRE FIRE WATER	You have more muscles than brain. Try sports.
FIRE FIRE AIR	With a great will and a good schooling you may succeed in art.
FIRE WATER FIRE	You are strong and tenacious. Try sports.
FIRE WATER WATER	You may be interested in the first and enjoy the latter, but do not expect great results.
FIRE WATER AIR	You may succeed in the first, without ever becoming a great star.
FIRE AIR FIRE	With real involvement and a good coach you can do well in sports.
FIRE AIR WATER	If you do not expect great results and world records, you may try sports.
FIRE AIR AIR	You have more sensitivity than strength. Try drama.
WATER FIRE FIRE	The stars suggest that you try a different career.
WATER FIRE WATER	Your inner nature is inclined to comedy. Try acting.
WATER FIRE AIR	Your nature is not made for the first, and your body not for the latter.
WATER WATER FIRE	You will have to wait for a long time, before you can succeed in acting.
WATER WATER WATER	The result will be mediocre in both.
WATER WATER AIR	Your success in an artistic career will be as brief as a flash of lightning.
WATER AIR FIRE	If you are undecided, try sports.
WATER AIR WATER	Abandon the idea. Enthusiasm is not enough in these hard careers.
WATER AIR AIR	An artistic career is more suitable

	for you, on the condition that you will be tenacious and hard working.
AIR FIRE FIRE	You will be successful only one time in a sports career.
AIR FIRE WATER	If in doubt, then try fine arts.
AIR FIRE AIR	Unforeseen events will take you away from the career you love.
AIR WATER FIRE	You can be successful in both.
AIR WATER WATER	You will succeed in an artistic career, and you will pay the price.
AIR WATER AIR	If you can bear tough sacrifice, you can be successful in sports.
AIR AIR FIRE	Your parents will make it impossible for you to follow these careers.
AIR AIR WATER	You will lose time in senseless projects. Think more deeply and realistically.
AIR AIR AIR	Your question is clearly useless, and you know why.

RESPONSES TO QUESTION #49

Is the person I am dealing with really sincere?

FIRE FIRE FIRE	You may find this quite strange, but yes the person is really sincere.
FIRE FIRE WATER	Yes. In any case keep your eyes constantly open in every situation.
FIRE FIRE AIR	Why do you doubt? Test the person and you will convince yourself.
FIRE WATER FIRE	For the duration of your relationship, you can trust this person completely.
FIRE WATER WATER	Yes. Stop investigating in such a

tormented way. You will reach no other conclusion.

FIRE WATER AIR Beware of this person's sincerity. Its nature is very elastic.

FIRE AIR FIRE This person is really sincere. Do not listen to those who try to make you change your mind.

FIRE AIR WATER Trust up to a certain point. Be wise and prudent.

FIRE AIR AIR Only partially. Do not torment yourself, instead believe only in what is convenient for you.

WATER FIRE FIRE The sincerity of this person is superior to your. Do not worry.

WATER FIRE WATER No. Pretend to be trustful, by acting in this way you will get more benefits.

WATER FIRE AIR Pretend to believe this person. This will help your personal strategies.

WATER WATER FIRE The nature of the person is really sincere. There is certain mistrust in regard to you and this causes a natural circumspection.

WATER WATER WATER The person is not very reliable and of limited sincerity.

WATER WATER AIR They are really sincere. Stop tormenting yourself with useless doubts.

WATER AIR FIRE The person reciprocates in equal measure your scarce sincerity.

WATER AIR WATER Certainly yes. Unfortunately your natural mistrust hinders you from appreciating it.

WATER AIR AIR Yes. Up to when your relations will overcome the agreed boundaries.

AIR FIRE FIRE Your mutual relations will improve when you show complete trust.

AIR FIRE WATER	They will be sincere until this is instrumental in helping a personal interest.
AIR FIRE AIR	Yes. The person will trust you more when their knowledge of you improves.
AIR WATER FIRE	Their expressed sincerity is only a mere calculation and not a true feeling.
AIR WATER WATER	Why should this person be sincere with you? You are being treated in kind.
AIR WATER AIR	You can count on it. The sincerity is spontaneous, instinctive and genuine.
AIR AIR FIRE	Yes. Unfortunately a rivalry will one-day damage your relationship.
AIR AIR WATER	They are really sincere. It is your responsibility to maintain this relationship on these terms.
AIR AIR AIR	My advice? Pretend to believe this person and observe the reactions. You will understand.

RESPONSES TO QUESTION #50

How will my affair end?

FIRE FIRE FIRE	It will end with a scandal extremely harmful to your status.
FIRE FIRE WATER	Happily. Feelings and sentiments of a superior nature will save you.
FIRE FIRE AIR	There will be no end. No illusions, so it is written.
FIRE WATER FIRE	It will end well, because you will

	save yourself at the last moment.
FIRE WATER WATER	How will it end? Not well, nor badly. An unforeseen event will destroy it.
FIRE WATER AIR	One day you will reap what you have so badly sown.
FIRE AIR FIRE	You will have to bear the risky weight for more moons to come.
FIRE AIR WATER	The answer is simple. You will lose the trust of the better person.
FIRE AIR AIR	Is not going to end. It will continue in secret for many more years.
WATER FIRE FIRE	What you call adultery will end rapidly, like a brief love affair.
WATER FIRE WATER	It will end abruptly because of mutual incompatibility.
WATER FIRE AIR	My advice? Return fast to the old lane. This will work much better for you.
WATER WATER FIRE	You will end up with an irregular union, much worse than before.
WATER WATER WATER	You will approach a scandal that will remarkably affect you.
WATER WATER AIR	You will break the relationship. The lover is worse than marriage.
WATER AIR FIRE	The stars are with you. It will end in the best possible way for you.
WATER AIR WATER	It will end bitterly, as it was only a physical attraction.
WATER AIR AIR	It will end insignificantly, and you will return to your original relationship.
AIR FIRE FIRE	The adultery will not last long. Too many fears will torment you.
AIR FIRE WATER	In a very negative way. What you have given will be for nothing.
AIR FIRE AIR	It will end naturally. Sex is not

	everything in a relationship.
AIR WATER FIRE	The answer is "a long and frustrating legal question will see the end of your relationship."
AIR WATER WATER	It will end in a childish way. You do not have the courage or the qualities to handle the situation.
AIR WATER AIR	The end will be logical and sad. An unthankful giving up.
AIR AIR FIRE	It will end soon and well. You will understand that the effort was not worth it.
AIR AIR WATER	It will end with a wise decision. Better to bite a bone than a stick.
AIR AIR AIR	It will end with a great and painful mutual deception.

RESPONSES TO QUESTION #51

What will be the result of my education?

FIRE FIRE FIRE	The result will confirm your talents and your efforts.
FIRE FIRE WATER	The result will surprise all those that did not trusted you.
FIRE FIRE AIR	Do not worry. The final result will compensate your great efforts.
FIRE WATER FIRE	The result will be mediocre and you will hardly succeed in finishing it. Pity.
FIRE WATER WATER	The result will oblige you to start a long voyage.
FIRE WATER AIR	The result will be proportional to your scarce efforts.
FIRE AIR FIRE	The result will be positive; but the

	time for success is still to come.
FIRE AIR WATER	The result will help you to improve your position.
FIRE AIR AIR	The result will be excellent. Unfortunately it will not help you to succeed in the business you have in mind.
WATER FIRE FIRE	The result will be negative. Evidently you are on the wrong path.
WATER FIRE WATER	Do not spend your energies in other activities and try to concentrate on the final result.
WATER FIRE AIR	The result will satisfy you and your special ambition.
WATER WATER FIRE	The positive result will be the right prize for your tenacious efforts.
WATER WATER WATER	The result will be inferior to your merits.
WATER WATER AIR	You will succeed at a later date. Others are passing you by.
WATER AIR FIRE	The result will not give you the satisfaction you desire and expect.
WATER AIR WATER	My advice: work harder and more seriously and the result will come.
WATER AIR AIR	You will have to face obstacles and rivalries of various natures.
AIR FIRE FIRE	Your weak and idle nature will delay positive results.
AIR FIRE WATER	The result will only leave you with a small deception. Pity.
AIR FIRE AIR	The result will be positive. You will make remarkable improvement right in time.
AIR WATER FIRE	The excellent result will increase envy you by others.
AIR WATER WATER	Do not worry. You will have to wait,

	but good results will finally arrive.
AIR WATER AIR	The result will give you glory and sadness at the same time.
AIR AIR FIRE	The result of your school education will be excellent, but your great efforts will be useless.
AIR AIR WATER	The success will be more rewarding from a moral, rather than from a financial point of view.
AIR AIR AIR	The result will be negative for you and your family.

RESPONSES TO QUESTION #52

Is my behavior wise and honest?

FIRE FIRE FIRE	It would certainly be so, if your nature would be really sincere and genuine.
FIRE FIRE WATER	You are vainly trying to convince yourself, with the inner supposition that it is true.
FIRE FIRE AIR	Retouch your inner character and the result will be what is expected.
FIRE WATER FIRE	Your family members do not think so, and they seem to be right.
FIRE WATER WATER	The answer is easy. Your attitude confirms the negative.
FIRE WATER AIR	Yes your behavior is so. You have to admit that it cost you great effort.
FIRE AIR FIRE	To the exterior world you deserve esteem. Your inner self knows that the real situation is different.
FIRE AIR WATER	Your behavior is wise for your selfishness, but not honest.

FIRE AIR AIR	Your behavior is wise and honest, because you have no other choice.
WATER FIRE FIRE	Your friends have a different opinion, and they are correct.
WATER FIRE WATER	Do not try to possess virtues that you do not have. It is difficult for you to make believe.
WATER FIRE AIR	Your behavior is honest, but certainly not wise. Think about that.
WATER WATER FIRE	Yes. But as soon as you have the opportunity, you will behave in a very different way.
WATER WATER WATER	These are qualities that do not match your inner nature.
WATER WATER AIR	Wise and honest because you don't have the courage to behave in a different way.
WATER AIR FIRE	Ask your conscience. The answer will be negative.
WATER AIR WATER	Now yes. But it is generous not to go back to your past.
WATER AIR AIR	It is wise and honest as long as this is convenient for you.
AIR FIRE FIRE	Yes, but it is better not to mention its elasticity.
AIR FIRE WATER	For your family members, yes. For your acquaintances, no.
AIR FIRE AIR	Yes. Unfortunately your innate ostentation is trying to show it off in an exaggerate way.
AIR WATER FIRE	I will be tempted to answer yes. But I understand that people who know you would not agree.
AIR WATER WATER	For the time being it is as you think. But in a short time it will change.
AIR WATER AIR	Wise and honest? Please reflect better and do not blaspheme.

AIR AIR FIRE	For the people that do not know you, yes. For your family members, no.
AIR AIR WATER	For you, yes, no doubt. But those who know you do not agree with you.
AIR AIR AIR	Yes, your behavior is wise and honest, and people like it.

RESPONSES TO QUESTION #53

Will I be able to find the financial help I need?

FIRE FIRE FIRE	Do not worry. You will find it in quantities even larger than your needs.
FIRE FIRE WATER	You will succeed. But not from the person you were counting on.
FIRE FIRE AIR	No. Ask for something less and you will be more successful the second time.
FIRE WATER FIRE	Yes, but you will have to concede in a regrettable way.
FIRE WATER WATER	Yes, but it will not be as easy as you initially thought.
FIRE WATER AIR	Not immediately. But with time you will be able to arrange for something positive.
FIRE AIR FIRE	Not through your friends. You will succeed thanks to your acquaintances.
FIRE AIR WATER	You will be able to find it, but under conditions absolutely not advantageous for you.
FIRE AIR AIR	Without presenting excellent

	credentials, it will be very difficult.
WATER FIRE FIRE	You will find the money you need, at the very last moment.
WATER FIRE WATER	Yes but not in the expected amount.
WATER FIRE AIR	You can count on it. Your friends are good and generous.
WATER WATER FIRE	Do not abandon the fight after the first negative sign. Continue with tenacity and one day you will succeed.
WATER WATER WATER	Partially yes. For the remaining you will have to fight hard, but you will be compensated for your efforts.
WATER WATER AIR	Ask astutely for a larger amount and you will find what you need.
WATER AIR FIRE	You can count on it. Your ability with eloquence will make your search easier.
WATER AIR WATER	You will find the money you need in an unexpected bizarre way.
WATER AIR AIR	Yes, but you will regret having asked that person.
AIR FIRE FIRE	You will find it by means of people you would have never expected.
AIR FIRE WATER	You can count on it. Your determined obstinacy will win over all obstacles.
AIR FIRE AIR	You will make it, through an innervating and frustrating vicious circle.
AIR WATER FIRE	You will succeed. Who could resist your special way of asking.
AIR WATER WATER	You will have to try different sources. Finally you will get what you need.
AIR WATER AIR	Yes, but thanks to a great effort.

	Your name does not enjoy great trust.
AIR AIR FIRE	You will succeed, but your proud head will have to bend to the floor.
AIR AIR WATER	You will certainly succeed. Your personality is trusted and esteemed.
AIR AIR AIR	Do not keep useless hopes, and try immediately some other way.

RESPONSES TO QUESTION #54

Will I be free of the person I am thinking of?

FIRE FIRE FIRE	One day yes. The stars will be on your side then.
FIRE FIRE WATER	Get rid of? Why? Think attentively and you will understand.
FIRE FIRE AIR	You will make it but not soon . Your nature is too weak.
FIRE WATER FIRE	You will succeed. But not by using your present system.
FIRE WATER WATER	Yes. A lucky circumstance will help you soon.
FIRE WATER AIR	You will succeed in a surprising way, in which you are not even thinking about.
FIRE AIR FIRE	Wait patiently. A voyage will be the right opportunity.
FIRE AIR WATER	You will succeed one day. But then you will not be interested anymore.
FIRE AIR AIR	No. And you know very well that all attempts will not succeed.
WATER FIRE FIRE	Do not reveal your secret goal and you will make it sooner.
WATER FIRE WATER	Yes. An unexpected event will

	resolve the problem drastically.
WATER FIRE AIR	Wait patiently. You will succeed in a certain time and with the right diplomacy.
WATER WATER FIRE	Can the turtle get rid of his shell? So it will be for you.
WATER WATER WATER	Yes. When the time for your departure arrives.
WATER WATER AIR	It is difficult. The person knows very well how to handle the situation.
WATER AIR FIRE	You will not succeed. Do not attempt to change your destiny. So it is written.
WATER AIR WATER	Can you face a bear without a gun? Then you can try.
WATER AIR AIR	You will succeed very soon, but it will be very expensive.
AIR FIRE FIRE	You will have to be as clever as the fox. This is the only way to achieve your goal.
AIR FIRE WATER	One day you will succeed. And you will bitterly regret it.
AIR FIRE AIR	You have a system: the law and a good lawyer.
AIR WATER FIRE	My advice: wait patiently and the person will leave on their own one day.
AIR WATER WATER	An unfortunate rivalry will do this favor to you, without realizing it.
AIR WATER AIR	Yes, with an act of force that will become dangerous to you.
AIR AIR FIRE	It will be very difficult. You have been fighting too long to tie this person to you.
AIR AIR WATER	Yes. Slowly, slowly and gradually defeating the granitic resistance.

AIR AIR AIR   Do not hold illusions in vain. This is going to be impossible on this Earth.

RESPONSES TO QUESTION #55

Do my relatives love me, and are they sincere?

FIRE FIRE FIRE
No illusions. The icy Siberian wind is like the look of their eyes.

FIRE FIRE WATER
Their sentiments are much better that you think. Reciprocate them in the same way.

FIRE FIRE AIR
They love you and they are sincere in their own way. Do not forget that each person has his own character.

FIRE WATER FIRE
You reap what you have sown. Look at the patient work of the good peasant.

FIRE WATER WATER
They have both love and sincerity for you. The problem is the lack of mutual understanding.

FIRE WATER AIR
Do not worry. When and if you need it, they will show the strength of their good feeling toward you.

FIRE AIR FIRE
The fireplace needs wood to make a good flame. Try to be the well-seasoned wood.

FIRE AIR WATER
No doubts. Wait patiently and you will touch with your hand the nature of their good feelings.

FIRE AIR AIR
There still is certain confusion in their heart. They still have to learn to know you well.

WATER FIRE FIRE
Somebody who is hostile to you,

	has put doubts in their minds. Wait, as time will be on your side.
WATER FIRE WATER	Be nice with them and particularly do not discriminate. We all have our own pride.
WATER FIRE AIR	Do not torment yourself. The feelings in your regard are sincere and benign.
WATER WATER FIRE	Sit down around the table with a bottle of good wine. Let's talk and drink. The bad feelings will disappear.
WATER WATER WATER	Certainly not. They envy you and hope you will fail socially as well as financially.
WATER WATER AIR	You are doing very little to improve your relationship. Try to modify your attitude first.
WATER AIR FIRE	Why all these doubts? They have shown in more than one occasion the value of their good sentiments.
WATER AIR WATER	They do not have a common agreement in your regard. This is partially your fault. Try to remedy this with improved behavior.
WATER AIR AIR	They are afraid of your character, and this slows down the strength of their feelings.
AIR FIRE FIRE	They are a little invading and meddlesome, but they really love you and are very sincere.
AIR FIRE WATER	Your question is out of place. Don't you see that you are at the center of their attention?
AIR FIRE AIR	Do not blame them. You are a bad merchant, because you are using two weighing systems at the same

	time.
AIR WATER FIRE	They love you and are sincere. They are prepared to sacrifice themselves to help you.
AIR WATER WATER	Visit them more often. They also need to know that you are being sincere and in love with them.
AIR WATER AIR	Be more respectful in their regard and they will show more clearly their sincere and good sentiments.
AIR AIR FIRE	Listen to them patiently and smile. Indifference is the enemy of love and sincerity.
AIR AIR WATER	Sometimes invite them to your home and show your hospitality. You will have another opportunity to understand their true feelings.
AIR AIR AIR	They are not sincere and do not love you. This is just the reciprocal feeling that you have for them.

RESPONSES TO QUESTION #56

Will I see improvements and/or promotions in my career?

FIRE FIRE FIRE	Do not feed impossible dreams. The blind goddess has forgotten you.
FIRE FIRE WATER	Shortly you will see an improvement, followed later on by the promotion.
FIRE FIRE AIR	Somebody has an interest in hiding your file, but if you persist in your good job, your time will come.
FIRE WATER FIRE	Show your personality. You have good qualities and you need to

	make sure than they are appreciated.
FIRE WATER WATER	Be content with the little expected. You know very well that you cannot have more.
FIRE WATER AIR	Work tenaciously and have faith. Improvements and a promotion will arrive.
FIRE AIR FIRE	You will find what you are looking for, but your pride will be hurt and you will suffer badly.
FIRE AIR WATER	Your luck is moving at a very slow speed, but it is moving. Be patient and the result will arrive.
FIRE AIR AIR	Your career is a squeezed lemon, but you are clever and will be capable of obtaining a few more drops.
WATER FIRE FIRE	You will obtain the desired promotion, but the financial improvement will disappoint you.
WATER FIRE WATER	You will obtain improvement and promotion through good and sincere friends.
WATER FIRE AIR	Do not worry. You will have to wait a few months but you will then get what you are waiting for.
WATER WATER FIRE	You will get what you are hoping for. Move fast, using the good relationships that can help you.
WATER WATER WATER	Absolutely not. You have too many enemies and this is working against you.
WATER WATER AIR	Continue to work and fight. Your success will come after a few more obstacles.
WATER AIR FIRE	The time is not ripe yet, but you are

	on the good road for improving and being promoted.
WATER AIR WATER	You will make it. Keep your projects to yourself and do not share them with your colleagues.
WATER AIR AIR	You will have what you desire. Unfortunately your character will take away the pleasure of enjoying it.
AIR FIRE FIRE	Certainly, using the method that you know so well: put oil on the wheels.
AIR FIRE WATER	What you want is not too far away. Many things are changing in your business environment.
AIR FIRE AIR	The stars will in your favor, but they also give you heavy responsibilities.
AIR WATER FIRE	You will count on good gifts from your luck, although you may not think it is the right time.
AIR WATER WATER	You will have what you want. But you will have to submit, and this will be very difficult for your character.
AIR WATER AIR	I suggest to contact a magician. I think you need his help.
AIR AIR FIRE	Certainly and a member of your family will be of great help.
AIR AIR WATER	You are more "thinking" than "acting." Try to move in the opposite way.
AIR AIR AIR	No, it is not possible. Don't you see that your tree is not bearing any fruits.

RESPONSES TO QUESTION #57

Should I change my job or business?

FIRE FIRE FIRE	No. It will be a great mistake and a major deception without remedy.
FIRE FIRE WATER	Think well. Change your system of work and bring in new and useful solutions.
FIRE FIRE AIR	This is certainly a good idea, but I suggest you to move to a foreign country.
FIRE WATER FIRE	You might, on condition of great sacrifices, very tough to face.
FIRE WATER WATER	Yes on one condition: change your place of residence.
FIRE WATER AIR	Yes. Decide fast and take the one that you did not want to do before.
FIRE AIR FIRE	It will be a useless risk. Instead work with more passion and motivation on your present job.
FIRE AIR WATER	Yes, follow your instinct. It will be difficult at the beginning but the results will arrive.
FIRE AIR AIR	Yes. Remember only to do what you are capable of doing well.
WATER FIRE FIRE	It is too early. First look at how certain aspects of your present business are developing.
WATER FIRE WATER	I do not see the advantages. Besides, this is the kind of activity you are really good at.
WATER FIRE AIR	You can certainly do that one day. But now it is not the right time.
WATER WATER FIRE	Why this question? You know very well that it is impossible and also consider that you are entering the

	evening of your life.
WATER WATER WATER	Absolutely not. In a few years you will be again in the same situation.
WATER WATER AIR	Why change? It's not going to be easy and you do not seem to have the required qualities.
WATER AIR FIRE	You can do it. Only be careful not to make the same mistake.
WATER AIR WATER	For certain reasons it will be a good idea. But do not underestimate the negative impact.
WATER AIR AIR	Your nature is very difficult to be satisfied. Why do you want to change? Try instead to modify your expectations.
AIR FIRE FIRE	I do not see how, unless you are prepared to destroy your family.
AIR FIRE WATER	Yes, but keep in mind that big organizations are not made for you.
AIR FIRE AIR	It will require a great effort, that neither your physical nor your psychological nature can bear.
AIR WATER FIRE	Certainly, but keep in mind that you will earn only thanks for hard work and efforts.
AIR WATER WATER	Think well. The water of the Great River overflows, but then returns in its banks and continues to flow as before.
AIR WATER AIR	Be tranquil and content with yourself. Your stars are good, but not outstanding.
AIR AIR FIRE	Why don't you change instead the type of people gravitating to you?
AIR AIR WATER	You are facing a crossroad. One road is good and the other bad, and you know it.

AIR AIR AIR	Why so much trouble? You will not be happy, even if you do it. The real problem is your own character.

RESPONSES TO QUESTION #58

Is my political and religious creed fair and correct?

FIRE FIRE FIRE	Is the thunderbolt that reduces to ashes your home fair? So is your case.
FIRE FIRE WATER	Before it was. Now you are losing yourself in obscure intellectualism and dangerous dead ends.
FIRE FIRE AIR	A creed? A faith? You are not capable of having either of them.
FIRE WATER FIRE	Your creed and your faith contain old mistakes. They both need to be reviewed.
FIRE WATER WATER	Your political creed will disappoint you. Reinforce your religious faith and you will find peace of mind.
FIRE WATER AIR	Beware of false prophets and their easy talking and promising.
FIRE AIR FIRE	Try to remain in the middle of the road with your common sense. This is the right place.
FIRE AIR WATER	You are right. Strengthen your will, as you will be faced with difficult tasks.
FIRE AIR AIR	Your old masters were right. Remove the bandage from your eyes.
WATER FIRE FIRE	You have no political creed nor religious faith. Your nature tends to

	follow the impossible dream.
WATER FIRE WATER	You change your mind too frequently. Try to anchor your thinking to a firm harbor.
WATER FIRE AIR	Do not worry. You are in the right direction. Try to stay on it forever.
WATER WATER FIRE	Credo? Faith? You have nothing there, only illusions.
WATER WATER WATER	You look like a tree's branch fallen in the Great River and being transported among the vortices.
WATER WATER AIR	Your nature is disconcerting and elastic. You have neither real creed nor faith.
WATER AIR FIRE	Right for Earth, wrong for Heaven.
WATER AIR WATER	You are right. But you have to prove it to your many detractors.
WATER AIR AIR	Stay within the boundaries and you will be right. When you exaggerate, you become wrong.
AIR FIRE FIRE	Be careful. You are only a puppet on the hand of your puppeteer.
AIR FIRE WATER	Your faith is tepid, and your creed uncertain. This is a real pity, because you are basically a very good person.
AIR FIRE AIR	Creed? Faith? Think again. You have great confusion.
AIR WATER FIRE	Yes and do not hide it. Keep your forehead high against the sun.
AIR WATER WATER	The water you are drinking is leaving you thirsty. Try other and better sources.
AIR WATER AIR	Return to the creed and faith of your ancestors and you will feel better.
AIR AIR FIRE	You are calling creed your desperate

	search for something to believe in.
AIR AIR WATER	Move away from those who are feeding your brain with cheap stuff. You will find your balance in yourself.
AIR AIR AIR	You are like a drunkard trying to find his house on a stormy night.

RESPONSES TO QUESTION #59

What do my parents think of me?

FIRE FIRE FIRE	Do not be surprised to hear the answer you already know: the consideration of your parents is not too good.
FIRE FIRE WATER	Your parents are expecting more determination and goodwill from you.
FIRE FIRE AIR	You are considered for what you are: your parents are getting old, but their sight is still good.
FIRE WATER FIRE	They count on you as a helping hand for their old age, and as a satisfaction for their efforts in rising you.
FIRE WATER WATER	Come back on the right track and their consideration will come back too.
FIRE WATER AIR	You are a problem without a solution for them. They do not understand you, but they love you.
FIRE AIR FIRE	They were counting on your intelligent behavior. Obviously you have deceived them.

FIRE AIR WATER	Their soul is simple. You are very important to them.
FIRE AIR AIR	You are a slave of sexual pleasures. Your parents have realized it and are suffering because of you.
WATER FIRE FIRE	Their consideration is natural and blind. They love you regardless to what you are doing.
WATER FIRE WATER	Your nature is ill. They know and realize your problem. Still, they love you.
WATER FIRE AIR	They are dreaming a little. They still consider you the child of years ago.
WATER WATER FIRE	Your parents are very concerned with your friendships, and they are not wrong.
WATER WATER WATER	You have made them older than their age. How should they consider you?
WATER WATER AIR	They consider you a weak person and are very concerned.
WATER AIR FIRE	You are the pupil of their eyes and the blood of their veins. You deserve it.
WATER AIR WATER	They know you are in bad hands and they are praying God to protect you.
WATER AIR AIR	Recently you have descended remarkably in their consideration.
AIR FIRE FIRE	They consider you a rebel. They are hoping in the good effect of time.
AIR FIRE WATER	Do not deceive them. They have made sacrifices for you and they count on your help.
AIR FIRE AIR	They consider you as you really are, very selfish and with little sentiment.

AIR WATER FIRE	They are very proud of your success and expect other outstanding results.
AIR WATER WATER	What consideration? The wind of your character is canceling all good intentions.
AIR WATER AIR	They consider you to be hypersensitive, influential and, above all, very controversial.
AIR AIR FIRE	They do not consider and do not judge. Their faith is great and they hope in a miracle.
AIR AIR WATER	They think you are a complex and difficult human being and they are seriously concerned.
AIR AIR AIR	Look at them for a few minutes. Their feelings are reflected in their tormented look.

RESPONSES TO QUESTION #60

Should I divorce?

FIRE FIRE FIRE	Wait patiently. Something will happen that will make your planned move useless.
FIRE FIRE WATER	Probably you should. But it is getting late, and your children will suffer a lot.
FIRE FIRE AIR	No. Do not listen to those who do not understand you feelings and your psyche.
FIRE WATER FIRE	Look at the anxious eyes of your children. The answer is there.
FIRE WATER WATER	It will be a mistake. Use your mind

	and your heart, not your impulsive emotions.
FIRE WATER AIR	Do not rush. Let the other part do the first move.
FIRE AIR FIRE	You can do it and you are right in doing it. But remember that nothing will change.
FIRE AIR WATER	No. It will only result in a long legal fight, without any good ending.
FIRE AIR AIR	No. Try instead to harmonize your characters using your mutual intelligence.
WATER FIRE FIRE	Keep in mind that your lawyer is acting with his interest in mind, and not yours.
WATER FIRE WATER	It is absolutely not the case. What you are facing is only a small sexual problem.
WATER FIRE AIR	You will find a great resistance from the other side. Think it over again.
WATER WATER FIRE	You should have done it at the right time. Now people will laugh at you.
WATER WATER WATER	If you think that is right to destroy a human being, then go ahead.
WATER WATER AIR	Wait before making a final decision. Investigate better. Your story has many unclear sides.
WATER AIR FIRE	Do not force events. There is a lot of mutual misunderstanding in your daily relations.
WATER AIR WATER	No and be patient. The person that you have married, in a special way, loves you.
WATER AIR AIR	Get rid of certain people living in your home. The divorce will not be necessary.
AIR FIRE FIRE	Think in regard to financial

interests. You are dealing with a very astute and determined person.

AIR FIRE WATER   It is not the case. Your union is not different from that of other people, who have learned to live together.

AIR FIRE AIR   No and be patient. One day you will thank me for this "unfair" suggestion.

AIR WATER FIRE   No. You will help the game of your rivals, Take time and you will see.

AIR WATER WATER   You should go ahead and do it. Keep only in mind that loneliness can be very sad.

AIR WATER AIR   No. Consider seriously also your mistakes and your bad moves.

AIR AIR FIRE   Your relatives will be too happy. Do not give them this satisfaction.

AIR AIR WATER   Slow down your temper. Wait: after the storm, the good weather always arrives.

AIR AIR AIR   Wait patiently. New events will change the situation for the best.

RESPONSES TO QUESTION #61

Is the person in my love affair in love with me?

FIRE FIRE FIRE   No illusions. It is only a short time love affair and at the end it will also be very expensive.

FIRE FIRE WATER   Yes but you have to be prepared. The old "triangle" will continue forever.

FIRE FIRE AIR   Yes. Unfortunately, because this person is facing an important decision in life and has a very weak will.

FIRE WATER FIRE — You are loved. But do not lose your head and do not underestimate the dangers of this affair.

FIRE WATER WATER — You are reciprocated only because of physical attraction. There are no real deep feelings.

FIRE WATER AIR — You are reciprocated deeply. Pity, because one day you will lose this person.

FIRE AIR FIRE — Yes. Beware, it is a dangerous relationship.

FIRE AIR WATER — Yes and the person is prepared to face fights and sacrifices with you.

FIRE AIR AIR — You are reciprocated. Do not underestimate the importance of rivalry.

WATER FIRE FIRE — Yes unfortunately. The possessive nature of this person will bring great problems to your life.

WATER FIRE WATER — Not exactly as you want. Your particular type of relationship does not offer more than this.

WATER FIRE AIR — Sincerely. Unfortunately this person does not realize your lack of loyalty.

WATER WATER FIRE — Yes but be careful. Somebody is controlling your moves, and has for a while.

WATER WATER WATER — Remove the bandage from your eyes. This person only loves your money.

WATER WATER AIR — Momentarily, as this person is frivolous and already thinking of new lovers.

WATER AIR FIRE — Useless question. Have you not had enough with recent events?

WATER AIR WATER	Similarly to your selfishness. Try to change and find happy medium.
WATER AIR AIR	Only superficially. Do not torment yourself. It is the character of this person that is unable to give more.
AIR FIRE FIRE	Your stars are protecting you beyond your merit. Realize that you do not deserve the love of this person.
AIR FIRE WATER	Very little and shortly you will realize it in a bitter manner.
AIR FIRE AIR	Unfortunately this person loves you too. And one day this mistake will cost both of you a great pain.
AIR WATER FIRE	Relatively. Only in relation to the generous gifts and the prosperity you are providing.
AIR WATER WATER	Yes but only for a very short period of time. This person cannot love for long.
AIR WATER AIR	Yes, but this affair is not going to last. New developments will change your destiny.
AIR AIR FIRE	Your relationship is complex like you and the person you love. An air of mystery will always be a companion to your feelings.
AIR AIR WATER	Yes, but do not oblige this person to make wrong moves, as you will regret it.
AIR AIR AIR	Think objectively. It is really impossible. The difference in age is too much of an obstacle.

RESPONSES TO QUESTION #62

What will my life be like when I retire?

FIRE FIRE FIRE	Loneliness and sadness will be with you in the last years of your life.
FIRE FIRE WATER	It will be not serene and tranquil because of your illness and your relatives.
FIRE FIRE AIR	Financially without worries. Very tormented because of a family situation.
FIRE WATER FIRE	Because of your character your last years will be lived in anxiety and torment.
FIRE WATER WATER	You will make new good friends, who will replace the love of your family.
FIRE WATER AIR	Good overall, as you will also find the opportunity for interesting part-time jobs.
FIRE AIR FIRE	Be careful with your lifestyle. You are at risk of not seeing retirement age.
FIRE AIR WATER	The warmth and loving care of your people will be with you and help you to end your life in serenity.
FIRE AIR AIR	You will reap what you sow. And unfortunately the harvest will be very meager.
WATER FIRE FIRE	Good with your health. A little troubled because of your financial situation.
WATER FIRE WATER	Wonderful, as you will finally realize that you are not alone.
WATER FIRE AIR	You will be loved and respected. Also you will feel that you are still

	useful.
WATER WATER FIRE	It should be not too bad. Unfortunately political and social events will disturb it.
WATER WATER WATER	You will be unhappy. You will feel like you are treated as a stranger.
WATER WATER AIR	Your life will improve. You will come down from your pedestal and envy will disappear.
WATER AIR FIRE	Your life will be serene. Financial security and good health will be your fine companions.
WATER AIR WATER	You will be a wise administrator of your savings.
WATER AIR AIR	Not too bad. Look after small illnesses and try to avoid worries.
AIR FIRE FIRE	If you do not learn how to live wisely, you will lose your life and your money.
AIR FIRE WATER	No fear. Your stars are protecting you. Your life will be long and serene.
AIR FIRE AIR	Change your character. This will help you greatly in your old days.
AIR WATER FIRE	Your life will be tranquil and serene. You will enjoy the results of your long efforts.
AIR WATER WATER	If you have the wise determination to forget your sex inclinations, your old age will be discreet.
AIR WATER AIR	In loneliness, in a way not different from the rest of your life.
AIR AIR FIRE	Those years will see ups and downs, exactly as those that you are experiencing now.
AIR AIR WATER	Your life will be better, because your family problems will finally be over.

AIR AIR AIR	You will be considered a useless thing, to be placed in the garret.

RESPONSES TO QUESTION #63

How will my gay friendship develop?

FIRE FIRE FIRE	Developments? None. The end will be unpleasant and you will be both responsible for.
FIRE FIRE WATER	So many, that at the end your life will be heavily influenced for a long time.
FIRE FIRE AIR	Do not forget that you have started it in the wrong way and so will be the development.
FIRE WATER FIRE	Little. Very few opportunities to get together.
FIRE WATER WATER	Your self destruction has finally found something to play with.
FIRE WATER AIR	In your destiny it is written that the end of the relation is close. Pity.
FIRE AIR FIRE	This new friend cannot satisfy your thirst. You will have to look for new sources.
FIRE AIR WATER	Not too bad. Ups and downs, due to your mutual differences of characters.
FIRE AIR AIR	Do not underestimate strong and old rivalries.
WATER FIRE FIRE	Mediocre developments that will not satisfy your feelings.
WATER FIRE WATER	You are very hungry. Your friendship will leave you so.
WATER FIRE AIR	Overall the development will be

	satisfactory. Be careful with regard to a rivalry.
WATER WATER FIRE	No serious developments. It is only a brief love story.
WATER WATER WATER	You will have to face a bitter and unpleasant delusion.
WATER WATER AIR	Your friendship is moving towards an impossible and dangerous direction.
WATER AIR FIRE	Very normal developments. Good sexual relations, but no more.
WATER AIR WATER	Think wisely. The eternal "triangle" will not reconcile with your character.
WATER AIR AIR	Developments? Troubles, misunderstandings, contrast, difficulties, but also some tenderness.
AIR FIRE FIRE	Be careful not to make imprudent moves. Tabloids may be interested in your story.
AIR FIRE WATER	Without a real goal. There is no mutual determination to proceed ahead.
AIR FIRE AIR	Great delusions. You remain a fantastic "dreamer."
AIR WATER FIRE	The relation will be constantly tormented by your incurable jealousy.
AIR WATER WATER	Your possessive nature will destroy all possible future developments.
AIR WATER AIR	Your relation is very superficial. Will end rapidly, as it has started.
AIR AIR FIRE	None. In your case sexual activity is not enough and will not fulfill your life.
AIR AIR WATER	Once again you will have to face a

AIR AIR AIR

burning delusion.
Be careful. The relation is becoming very dangerous.

BIBLIOGRAPHY

Yliodor, the Monk	*The Saint Devil*	Moscow, 1920
S.P. Beletski	*Grigori Rasputin*	Moscow, 1923
Fulop-Miller Rene	*Rasputin*	London, 1928
M.V. Rodzyanko	*The Sign of Rasputin*	Philpot, 1927
Gian Dauli	*Rasputin*	Milan, 1934
Felix Yussupoff	*Rasputin's Orgies*	Putnam, 1953
Marie Rasputin	*Rasputin, My Father*	Paris, 1966
Anonymous	*The Great Muzhik*	no date

Czar Nicholas II and Czarina Alexandra
Official engagement photograph, April 1894

Czarevich Alexei

The Romanov family
Taken to mark the 300th anniversary of the Romanov dynasty, 1913

The children of Nicholas II and Alexandra
From left to right: Maria, Tatiana, Anastasia, Olga, Alexei

Czarina Alexandra and Alexei

The starets *Rasputin*

*From left to right: Rasputin, the Bishop Hermogenes
and the monk Yliodor*

*Rasputin with Major General Putyatin
and Colonel Lotman, c. 1904*

Rasputin with some supporters, 1914

Prince Felix Yusupov

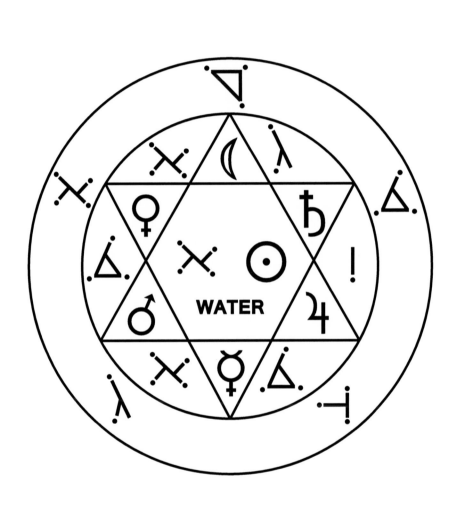
WATER

Leopoldo Benassi, *Prof. Manteia* (1908-1975)

Leopoldo Benassi, who went by the pen name "Manteia," was an Italian who lived in Rome. Manteia dedicated his life to the study of occultism and divination, always with the intention of writing about the life of famous clairvoyants.

He published several successful books on such fascinating subjects as the *Prophecies of Nostradamus*, the *Life of Cagliostro* and *The Oracle of Rasputin*.

His most revered book, *The Oracle of Rasputin* is an ancient script attributed to the controversial Russian clairvoyant Rasputin and was discovered by Manteia in a rare encounter with a mysterious gentleman. Manteia deciphered the text written in Old Russian and translated it into Italian.

Manteia was a passionate chiromancer and an accredited member of Esoteric Academies and Universities, and was determined to demonstrate that chiromancy is a science fighting against those rascals that deceived the profession.

He was much respected and admired, and was always referred to as a *chirosopher* from the Greek *kheir*, hand and *sofós*, sapient.

Paolo Benassi

The only son of Manteia, Paolo was born in Italy and lived with his father until when he married his wife Paola and moved to Florida as Vice President of a well known cruise line.

He still remembers when as a child the individuals would visit his father, the chirosopher, for advice and he felt awe by how impressed they were with Manteia's palmistry know-how and understanding of human nature.

Growing up Paolo would on occasion help his father proofread his books, and this ultimately became a great opportunity to personally witness Manteia's passion and dedication.

After his father's death, Paolo decided to translate his most successful book *The Oracle of Rasputin* to ensure that Manteia's reputation continues to live on, and that his works can be enjoyed by many more readers to come.

KERUBIM PRESS

WWW.KERUBIMPRESS.COM

FOLLOW US ON TWITTER
WWW.TWITTER.COM/KERUBIMPRESS

LIKE US ON FACEBOOK
WWW.FACEBOOK.COM/KERUBIMPRESS

Lightning Source UK Ltd.
Milton Keynes UK
UKOW050610170213

206359UK00004B/17/P